BIBLICAL PROPHECY
UNVEILED
PROPHECY MADE EASY

Indeed, the Sovereign Lord never does anything
until he reveals his plans to his servants the prophets.
—Amos 3:7

MICHAEL F. ELMORE, MD

WESTBOW
P R E S S®
A DIVISION OF THOMAS NELSON
& ZONDERVAN

Scripture quotations taken from the New American Standard Bible® (NASB), Copyright © 1960, 1962, 1963, 1968, 1971, 1972, 1973, 1975, 1977, 1995 by The Lockman Foundation. Used by permission. www.Lockman.org

Scriptures Taken from the King James Version of the Bible.

Scripture quotations marked (NIV) are taken from the Holy Bible, New International Version®, NIV®. Copyright © 1973, 1978, 1984, 2011 by Biblica, Inc.™ Used by permission of Zondervan. All rights reserved worldwide. www.zondervan.com The "NIV" and "New International Version" are trademarks registered in the United States Patent and Trademark Office by Biblica, Inc.™

Scripture quotations marked (NLT) are taken from the Holy Bible, New Living Translation, copyright ©1996, 2004, 2015 by Tyndale House Foundation. Used by permission of Tyndale House Publishers, Inc., Carol Stream, Illinois 60188. All rights reserved.

Scripture quotations marked MSG are taken from THE MESSAGE, copyright © 1993, 1994, 1995, 1996, 2000, 2001, 2002 by Eugene H. Peterson. Used by permission of NavPress. All rights reserved. Represented by Tyndale House Publishers, Inc.

WestBow Press books may be ordered through booksellers or by contacting:

WestBow Press
A Division of Thomas Nelson & Zondervan
1663 Liberty Drive
Bloomington, IN 47403
www.westbowpress.com
1 (866) 928-1240

ISBN: 978-1-9736-2989-4 (sc)
ISBN: 978-1-9736-2988-7 (e)

Print information available on the last page.

WestBow Press rev. date: 6/25/2018

To my nephew Matthew Teeple, who was the inspiration for this book; to my daughter, Kimberly, who helped guide me in the writing; and to Pastor Darrell Stout, who planted the seed of desire within me to understand prophecy.

Contents

Acknowledgments

I want to thank all the people I worked with at WestBow Press for their help in making this book a reality.

Introduction

What God has said He will do, He has done, He is doing, and He will do!
You don't need to live in fear of the last days. You can
be prepared and excited about Jesus's return.

There is a tremendous interest in the so-called "last days." Just look at all the movies that deal with the apocalypse or civilizations that exist on earth after some form of global destruction. At the same time, this interest does not always lead to a hunger to study biblical prophecy. Many people turn away, thinking the subject is too complicated and too confusing due to so many differing opinions. This leads to ignorance and leaves many hiding their heads in the sand like a fearful ostrich. I believe it is not that difficult to gain a basic understanding of what is to come. God, through His prophets, has revealed much. He does not want us living in fear of the end times; in fact, quite the opposite.

The most significant reason to study the last days is to be prepared for the Second Coming of Jesus Christ. The early church was often under intense persecution, and the information Jesus and the apostles provided was designed to educate and encourage believers in the midst of persecution. Jesus gave several signs so believers would be prepared for the judgments coming on the earth. Despite the persecution believers may experience, God assures believers that they will be sealed and protected from these judgments. I hear people ask, "What will happen to my family and me if we don't take the mark of the beast?" But what they should be asking is, "What will happen to us if we are not sealed with the mark of God?"

When we hear terms like the *tribulation* and the *great tribulation*, it's natural to become fearful. However, Jesus gave us several signs to watch for so we will be prepared for the end. Unbelievers will be living as if everything is fine, just as they did in the days of Noah when the flood came suddenly and surprised them. Noah, however, was given instructions by God. He knew what was coming and how to prepare. Noah and his family were ready when the judgment of God came upon the earth. Similarly, the end-time prophecies have been given to us so we can be prepared and ready too.

God wants us to not only be prepared for His Son's Second Coming but also to live in a state of excitement and anticipation. The early church lived, believing Jesus's return was imminent, and God wants us to live that way also. Scripture clearly states that no one, not even Jesus, knows exactly when God will send Him back. So when you hear people claiming to know and making predictions regarding when Jesus will return, you can be certain of one thing: They don't know!

What Prophecy Is and Isn't

Most people seem to think of prophecy as foretelling or predicting the future. That is certainly one aspect of biblical prophecy, but an equally important function of the prophets was instructing and exhorting people to turn from their sins and back to God. Often those functions and their divinely inspired messages were intertwined.

Recently my nephew expressed his confusion with much of biblical prophecy and asked me, "Why isn't there a book that isn't too long that somehow explains the many prophecies in a simple way?" I thought that was a very good question. I had been studying biblical prophecy for years, and for many of those years I was just as confused as he was. Similarly, many Christians who read through the Bible every year have told me that they get bogged down in books like Isaiah and Jeremiah, as well as the books of the minor prophets. I have often thought it doesn't have to be this way! This brief volume is an attempt to make biblical prophecy understandable and to put many of the prophecies in their proper context, contextually, geographically, and historically. It would be impossible for me to cover all the prophecies, but I will touch on the ones I believe are the most significant. With a basic understanding of prophecy, I believe these books will open up to readers and become incredibly insightful and even exciting.

At times when reading Old Testament prophecies, it can be very frustrating to understand exactly what events the prophet is speaking about and when they are occurring. The prophets had a way of speaking of relatively current events and interweaving them with more distant future events, all within a verse or two. Sometimes the prophets understood the meaning of their prophecies, but on many occasions they did not. They simply wrote down what God gave them to say or what they saw in their dreams or visions. Some of the Old Testament prophecies are quoted in the New Testament, which provides more information, helping us to more fully understand them.

The Bible is considered the best-selling book of all time, with over five billion copies sold. It was written over almost fifteen hundred years by more than forty authors and in many different settings. There are two parts to the Bible:

The Old Testament (OT) includes thirty-nine books consisting of the Pentateuch (Torah), the historical books, the so-called "wisdom" books, and the prophets.

The New Testament (NT) includes twenty-seven books consisting of four narratives of Jesus's life, teaching, death, and resurrection called Gospels, the Acts of the apostles, twenty-one letters written to various early churches, and the book of Revelation, also called the Apocalypse of John.

Since there were four major prophets (Isaiah, Jeremiah, Ezekiel, and Daniel) and twelve minor prophets, if we are confused and unable to understand their messages, that represents a significant portion of the Old Testament. Most important, many times their messages are essential to a proper understanding of much of the New Testament and the prophecies that unfold today. Unfortunately, many theologians teach that God is finished with the nation of Israel. If they were fully acquainted with the major and minor prophets' messages, they would never believe this. The clear message these prophets present is an unmistakable recurrent theme that one day God will bring back the Jews that are scattered throughout the world, and they will live in the land of Israel in peace and safety. The present state of Israel was established in 1948, and Jews from all over the world have been coming to resettle there. But this is just the beginning. They are not living in safety but rather under the constant threat of war from the surrounding Arab nations. But God promised, as we will see, that this will not last forever. God is always faithful to His covenants. Through the restoration of His people in the Promised Land, God will reveal Himself to not only His people but to the entire world. The world will finally see and acknowledge Yahweh as the one true and only God.

The Bible was written in three languages. Most of the OT was written in Hebrew (the language of the Israelites), and some parts were written in Aramaic (the language of the Near East from the sixth century BC through the fourth century BC). Around 250 BC, the OT was translated into Greek for those Jews who no longer spoke Hebrew. This translation is called the Septuagint. Almost all of the NT was written in Greek, which was the international language at the time of Christ. Perhaps one of the most incredible aspects of the Bible is that it has been preserved for us throughout time with an accuracy no other ancient literature can claim. This fact speaks to God's supervision and preservation of His Word over time. You would think that being written by so many different authors over so great a period of time and in three different languages that there would be significant diversity regarding the many topics the Bible addresses. However, quite the opposite is true. Considerable harmony exists throughout the Bible, which presents one overall important story. It is the story of God's love for man and His plan of redemption through His Son, Jesus Christ, the Messiah. The prophets' messages reveal this to us repeatedly.

Some time ago one of my daughters asked me this question: "Dad, what is the difference between prophecy and fortune-telling?" I told her there is a big difference. Prophecy is God's revelation to man regarding future events. Fortune-telling is the ancient black art of divination, which is an occult practice used to gain hidden information or insight on future events by invoking demonic spirits. God strictly forbids all such activity, as specified in Deuteronomy 18:9–12. Information obtained from demonic sources is often misleading, wrong, and/or deceptive. Satan uses these occult practices to influence and control, which are inconsistent with the will of God for our lives.

Prophetic Themes

People are often confused about why God does one thing or another. There are definite prophetic themes throughout the Bible, and a basic understanding of these themes reveals God's nature and how He thinks and operates. Here a few of the prophetic themes:

1. Judgment. This is punishment for wickedness and pride. God uses punishment hoping people will turn from their sinful ways and turn to Him.
2. Discipline. In the same way parents discipline their children because they love them and want the best for them, so God disciplines us, His children, to get us back on the right track.
3. Restoration. Virtually always intertwined with discipline is the promise of restoration. In other words, the discipline will not last forever, and God has better plans on the other side of discipline.
4. Sovereignty of God. The judgments of God always serve a positive purpose. Nations and evil forces may think and act like they are independent of God, but they are all accountable to God. As history has shown, they continually are being overthrown. Additionally, with the Second Advent of Christ, all evil will be overthrown with the establishment of His kingdom. The Prince of Peace will bring peace on earth.
5. Warning and protection. Through the prophets, God often warned His people of future problems, such as famine, to protect them so they could be prepared for what was coming.
6. Messianic. Throughout the Bible, we see the theme of the coming of the Messiah. In the Old Testament, there are many prophecies concerning the first coming of Jesus Christ. In both the Old Testament and New Testament, there are also many prophecies regarding Jesus's Second Coming.

Through these powerful themes, God reveals His incredible love for mankind, played out in real-life situations.

God's Strategy

God has a marvelous plan for the restoration of all things. Because we live within the framework of time, which God created for us, we often limit God, trying to constrain Him within that framework. However, God lives outside of time. That's why when Moses asked God His name, God replied, "I Am" (Exodus 3:14). God always has been, is, and always will be. Of course it's hard for us to wrap our heads around this because we are finite, and God is infinite. Similarly, when God speaks of our calling and predestination, many struggle to understand these concepts.

But the apostle Paul stated, "And we know that all things work together for good to them that love God, to them who are the *called* according to his purpose. For whom he did *foreknow,* he also did *predestinate* to be conformed to the image of his Son, that he might be the firstborn among many brethren. Moreover whom he did *predestinate,* them he also *called*: and whom he *called,* them he also justified: and whom he justified, them he also glorified" (Romans 8:28–30, emphasis added).

The obvious question is, "Since God created me with a free will, how could He call, foreknow, and predestinate me without interfering with my free will?" The answer lies in understanding who God is outside of time. Jesus identified Himself as follows: "I am Alpha and Omega, the beginning and the end, the first and the last" (Revelation 22:13). God is omniscient, which means He knows everything. Since He exists outside the framework of time and knows everything that has happened, is happening, and will happen, He knows how we will respond to the many choices given to us. He knows who will respond to His mercy and grace and who will not. From before the creation of the world, He has always known what great leaders of nations would do in all situations. What is so amazing is that He has woven and continues to weave all our actions into the mosaic of human history for His purposes, without ever violating our free will.

God has revealed His ultimate strategy and plan to us. Paul said this to the church at Ephesus: "And this is the plan: At the right time he will bring everything together under the authority of Christ—everything in heaven and on earth" (Ephesians 1:10 NLT).

The apostle Peter said this about Jesus, the Messiah: "For he must remain in heaven until the time for the final restoration of all things, as God promised long ago through his holy prophets" (Acts 3:21 NLT).

God's strategy is clear. He is going to restore everything and in the process put everything under the authority and control of His Son, Jesus. God gives each of us the opportunity to play a role in His plans and to be involved in changing the future. Our choices come with consequences, with effects for good or evil. There are times when God is searching for those who will intercede and "stand in the gap" for His purposes: "And I sought for a man among them, that should make up the hedge, and stand in the gap before me for the land, that I should not destroy it: but I found none" (Ezekiel 22:30).

The Bible says that God is continually searching for men and women whose hearts belong completely to Him in order that He can strongly support them (2 Chronicles 16:9). God does not need our help; He could do everything on His own, but He chooses to do otherwise. He is looking for those of us who will partner with Him to accomplish His purposes.

Outline of This Book

Without a knowledge of Israel's history, biblical prophecy has no context and makes no sense. So in part 1, I start by providing a timeline for Jewish history in the context of significant world history events. You may wish to read this or simply use it as a reference tool.

In part 2, I explain the geography of the Bible, which is essential to understanding the history of Israel.

Part 3 is a short synopsis of some of the historical events recorded in the Old Testament. It gives an overview of Jewish history. This is necessary in order to understand the context in which the prophecies were made.

In part 4, I pay particular attention to messianic prophecies, most of which have been fulfilled. The specificity with which many of these prophecies were made about Jesus, the Messiah, hundreds of years before His birth, is simply astounding.

Finally, in part 5, I cover the part of the book of Revelation that concerns the tribulation period, and I have integrated many of the relevant Old Testament prophecies where they fit. I also have gone to great depths to provide supplementary material that helps to explain the prophecies.

Once you have read this book, I doubt you will ever read your daily newspaper the same again! Remember what the prophet Amos said: "Indeed, the Sovereign Lord never does anything until he reveals his plans to his servants the prophets" (Amos 3:7 NLT).

Throughout my life, I always have been engaged in some form

of teaching. Early in my practice years as a gastroenterologist, I was an instructor in biochemistry at the Indiana University School of Medicine and later an associate clinical professor of medicine with a clerkship in gastroenterology and nutrition. Several years ago I published a book titled *The Ancient Path: Rediscovering Manhood,* and over the next eight years, I used it to mentor fifty men, helping them to grow spiritually and become the men God intended. My purpose in writing this book on prophecy is also to educate my readers but not just about understanding prophecy. My experience has shown me that people have many questions about various issues in the Bible. So at various points in this book, I have taken the time to answer many of these questions. Here are a few of the questions on which I chose to focus:

1. I don't understand all the covenants in the Bible. What was their purpose?
2. Why did the Israelites have to wander for forty years in the wilderness after they left Egypt before entering the Promised Land?
3. Of all the nations on earth, why did God choose Israel to be the chosen people?
4. Polygamy was rampant in the Old Testament. What was God's position on that?
5. What was the purpose of circumcision in the Old Testament? And what does the term "spiritual circumcision," used in the New Testament, mean?
6. Some of my friends are Jewish, and they hold a seder meal once a year. Does this have any relevance to Christianity?
7. Whatever happened to the ark of the covenant? Where is it, and will it resurface at some point?
8. I don't completely understand the concept of a tithe. Is tithing optional or mandatory?
9. The modern state of Israel was established in 1948. Does the Bible attribute any significance to this?
10. The second temple in Jerusalem was destroyed in AD 70 by the Romans. Will a third temple be built? And if so, why?

11. Some people believe that the Old Testament sacrificial system will be reinstituted in Israel. Jesus's death on the cross accomplished everything for us; why would this be necessary?
12. I heard something about the ashes of a red heifer being used for water for purification. That sounds really strange! What's that all about?
13. I hear people talk about a so-called rapture. What is it, and when will it occur?

I have quoted many scripture verses in this book and have used the King James Version (KJV) for most of them. I love the eloquence and flow of the KJV, yet it can sometimes be difficult to understand. So at times, I have used alternative translations when I felt necessary. If you have difficulty understanding one or more verses I have quoted in the KJV, I suggest you use your favorite translation of the Bible and follow along. Additionally, some scripture citations simply are too lengthy, so in those cases I have indicated the verses in the Bible to read.

Are There Prophets Today?

Another frequent question is, "Are there modern-day prophets?" The apostle Paul made it clear that the apostles and prophets were the foundation of the church, and Jesus Christ is the cornerstone (Ephesians 3:20). In the church today, one side takes the theological position that since we have the complete canon of scripture, prophets are no longer needed. Others disagree. I do believe there are men and women who function as modern-day prophets, exhorting believers to forsake sinful ways and live godly lives, but I do not believe they add additional future prophecies to scripture. Jesus strictly forbade this (Revelation 22:18–19). The function of prophets was to deliver divinely inspired revelations of God. These centered around three issues:

1. Explaining God's will regarding religious and moral issues
2. Foretelling future events
3. Expounding on truth that usually had something to do with the character of God

In the early church, people were never to just accept the words of a prophet. Rather, they were instructed to always test the prophets and their words to see if they were from God (1 John 4:1; 1 Thessalonians 5:20–21). Here were the tests to be used:

1. A prophet's message never contradicted scripture (1 Corinthians 14:29; 2 Peter 1:20–21).
2. A prophet's predictions had to come true 100 percent of the time (Jeremiah 28:9).
3. The life of a prophet had to be one of integrity. Jeremiah constantly exposed false prophets as living a lie; that is, living lives of hypocrisy (Jeremiah 23:14).
4. A prophet always presented God's truth, even when it offended people.

I would also like to add a fifth test in our present-day atmosphere. A prophet is a prophet and not a profit! A person who profits substantially from his or her prophecies is likely not of God.

Goals of This Book

After you have read this book, I expect you to experience the following:

1. Live with great anticipation and excitement, looking forward to Jesus's return, rather than living in a state of fear and apprehension.
2. Understand clearly what prophecy is and God's intended purpose for it.
3. Have a basic understanding of prophecy from both the Old Testament and New Testament perspectives.
4. Comprehend scripture with a depth not previously experienced.

It is my hope that with the understanding of prophecy you receive, you will be able to build upon this foundation to explore other prophecies on your own.

PART 1
Jewish Historical Timeline

3000–2000 BC—Egyptian Empire

2919 BC—Noah

2166 BC—Abram

2091 BC—Abraham entered Canaan.

2066 BC—The birth of Isaac.

2006 BC—The birth of Jacob and Esau.

1929 BC—Jacob fled to Haran.

1898 BC—Joseph was sold into slavery.

1885 BC—Joseph ruled Egypt.

1805 BC—Joseph died.

1526 BC—The birth of Moses.

1446 BC—The exodus from Egypt.

1445 BC—God gave the Ten Commandments.

1450–1410 BC—The Levitical laws.

1450–1410 BC—The book of Numbers.

1407–1406 BC—The book of Deuteronomy.

1406 BC—The Hebrews entered the Promised Land.

1375–1050 BC—The reign of the judges in Israel.

1105 BC—The birth of Samuel.

1050 BC—Saul became Israel's first king (the book of 1 Samuel).

1010 BC—David became Israel's king (the book of 2 Samuel); the united kingdom known as Israel.

970 BC—Solomon became Israel's king.

930 BC—The kingdom of Israel was divided into the northern kingdom of Israel and the southern kingdom of Judah.

875 BC—Elijah prophesied in Israel.

874 BC—Ahab became Israel's king.

855–840 or 627–586 BC—Obadiah the prophet.

848 BC—Elisha prophesied in Israel.

835 BC—Joash became Judah's king.

835–796—Joel the prophet.

785–760 BC—Jonah the prophet.

760 BC—Amos the prophet.

746 BC—Hosea the prophet.

743 BC—Tiglath-Pileser III of Assyria invaded Israel.

739–700—Isaiah the prophet.

740–687 BC—Micah the prophet.

721 BC—Assyrian captivity; Samaria, capital of the northern kingdom was destroyed; the "times of the Gentiles" began.

701 BC—Sennacherib of Assyria besieged Jerusalem.

663–612 BC—Nahum the prophet.

640 BC—Josiah became Judah's king.

640–621 BC—Zephaniah the prophet.

627–586 BC—Jeremiah the prophet.

612 BC—Nineveh, the Assyrian capital, was destroyed.

612–589 BC—Habakkuk the prophet.

609 BC—Battle of Megiddo; the defeat of Judah by Egypt, in which King Josiah was killed; Judah became a vassal state of Egypt.

605 BC—Battle of Carchemish; the decisive Babylonian victory over Egypt and Assyria.

605–536 BC—Daniel the prophet.

586 BC—Babylonian captivity; Judah (southern kingdom) fell to Babylon and Jerusalem was destroyed.

562 BC—King Nebuchadnezzar of Babylon died.

539 BC—Babylon overthrown by Cyrus of Persia.

538 BC—First Jewish exiles returned to Jerusalem, led by Zerubbabel.

520 BC—Haggai the prophet.

520–480 BC—Zechariah the prophet.

515 BC—Second temple completed in Jerusalem.

479 BC—Esther became queen of Persia.

458 BC—Ezra led second return to Jerusalem.

445 BC—Nehemiah led third return and rebuilt the wall of Jerusalem.

430 BC—Malachi the prophet.

390 BC—Aramaic began to replace Hebrew as the Jewish language.

331 BC—Greek Empire; Alexander the Great (356–323 BC) was king of the ancient Greek kingdom of Macedon. He succeeded his father, Philip II (of the Agread dynasty), to the throne at age twenty and over the next ten years engaged in an unprecedented military campaign, creating one of the largest empires of the ancient world, stretching from Greece to northwestern India. He died in Babylon in 323 BC. After his death, a series of civil wars tore the empire apart, resulting in several states ruled by the Diadochi (from the Greek *diadochus*—successors), made up of Alexander's surviving generals and heirs.

Seleucid dynasty (named after a Greek Macedonian family)

Seleucus I Nicator 320–281 BC

Antiochus I Soter 281–261 BC

169 BC—The temple in Jerusalem was plundered by Antiochus IV Ephiphanes 175–163 BC—He took Jerusalem when the Jews resisted him, and he rededicated the temple to Zeus, sacrificed swine in the temple ("abomination of desolation"), and made the observance of Hebrew law punishable by death. During this time, the rise of the *Decopolis* (Greek: "ten cities") occurred, which included Gerasa in Jordan, Scythopolis in Israel (the only city west of the Jordan), Hippos in Israel (Golan Heights), Gadara in Jordan, Pella in Jordan, Philadelphia (modern-day Amman, the capital of Jordan), Capitolias (today, Beit Ras in Jordan), Canatha (in Syria), Raphana (in Jordan) and Damascus (capital of modern Syria). It was a center of Greek and Roman culture in a region that was otherwise ancient Semitic-speaking peoples (Nabataeans, Arameans, and Judeans).

The Seleucids ruled until 63 BC.

Antigonid dynasty—Antigonus I Monophthalmus was a general of Alexander the Great who ruled from 306 to 168 BC.

Ptolemaic dynasty (a Macedonian Greek family)—Ptolemy was one of the *somatophylakes* (bodyguards) who served as one of Alexander the Great's generals and was appointed satrap of Egypt after Alexander's death in 323 BC. He ruled from 305 to 283 BC. There were twelve Ptolemys, followed by two Cleopatras, who ruled. The Ptolemaic dynasty ruled Judea until 198 BC.

165 BC—Maccabean period; Judas Maccabeus, a priest of the Hasmonean family, led a Jewish rebellion and defeated the Seleucids. He took complete control of Jerusalem and rededicated the temple. This event is celebrated annually by the Jews as *Hanukkah,* known as the *Feast of Dedication* in the New Testament (John 10:22).

The Hasmoneans were Jewish kings who ruled from 143 to 63 BC. Subsequently, bitter conflict occurred between the Hasmoneans and Pharisees, a rural priestly sect that propounded strict observance of Hebrew religious tradition. In the struggle, both factions asked for help from the new political/military power of Rome.

First century—Petra-based Nabataean Empire at its height.

73 BC—Herod the Great was born in and grew up in Judea. His father was Arab and his mother an Edomite, but he was raised as a Jew (but considered a half Jew). Later the Roman senate named him king of Judea, due to his loyalty to Rome.

63 BC—Cleopatra was born and subsequently inherited the throne when her father died in 51 BC.

63 BC—Roman legions under Pompey conquered Jerusalem; Roman governors, called procurators, ruled.

48 BC—Gaius Julius Caesar became sole ruler of the Roman Empire. He was assassinated in 44 BC. He wanted power in order to do good, and he believed in the principle of clemency. He said, "Let this be a new way of conquering, that our strength and our security lie in pity and generosity." He ruled as an autocratic divine king, which led to his assassination by reactionary senators in 44 BC. They preferred freedom to domination. He was married to Cleopatra, who fled with their son to Egypt.

44 BC—Augustus Caesar (Octavius) became emperor of the Roman Empire. He died in AD 14. He believed that direction without freedom was tyranny, and freedom without direction was anarchy. Antony was his most popular general. Antony later withdrew to Egypt and married Cleopatra.

37 BC—Herod the Great was made king of Judea by the Romans.

31 BC—Octavian crushed Antony and Cleopatra at the Battle of Actium and was subsequently given the title *Augustus* (meaning "worthy of reverence"). Herod rushed to Octavian at the Isle of Rhodes and swore allegiance to him. Octavian was impressed and confirmed Herod as king of Judea and added other territories to his realm. Herod was generous to his

subjects in times of famine and natural disasters. He undertook amazing building projects, including the northern palace at Masada, rebuilding the temple in Jerusalem, the port city of Caesarea, the Herodian Antonia fortress, and several other fortresses.

Roman Empire—Ruled 27 BC through AD 395

20 BC—Herod began remodeling the temple in Jerusalem.

5 BC—Augustus had the ability to make a moral conquest of nations, extending freedom to the annexed peoples. He became the emperor and judge of the nations from Britain to India. He created order out of chaos, an age of blessing such as the war-ridden world had never seen. He was believed to be the world's savior, and the advent celebrations began with the Advent Proclamation: "Salvation is to be found in no other save Augustus, and there is no other name given to men in which they can be saved." But the Roman advent message promised more than any emperor could fulfill.

6/5 BC—Jesus Christ was born (Anno Domini). It was in the context of seeing Augustus as the savior of the world that Jesus came as the real Savior of the world.

At the request of Quirinius, a census was carried out in Palestine as a basis for levying imperial taxes. Herod was the legal functionary of Augustus and sent the taxes on to Caesar, but he also enacted taxes of his own, which he collected with greed and brutality. A number of years later, Jesus was questioned about this tax money. Jesus asked for a denarius because of the many coins circulated at the time. It was the prescribed coin for taxation purposes (Mark 12:16; Luke 20:24; Matthew 22:19). The denarius they showed him had Tiberius Caesar on the coin (the emperor shown on the coin had to be the ruling emperor). The coin was a symbol of both power (imperial supremacy, the ruler's dominance, and fiscal policy) and the cult of divinity (implying Olympian divinity deserving of worship). Jesus told them it was not improper for Caesar to demand that what was his be given back to him, but what was exclusively God's should be given back to God. Jesus made it clear that since His questioners had accepted the imperial denarii in payment, it meant that they, the people of God, had accepted its subjugation to the Roman Empire; that is, by accepting and using the imperial money, they had benefited financially, economically, and legally from the order of the empire. Hence, they owed the tax and should pay it. Jesus was affirming the *Imperium Romanum* as a true succession of the prophetic and apocalyptic theology of history. Jeremiah 27:5–8 (NLT) states,

> With my great strength and powerful arm I made the earth and all its people and every animal. I can give these things of mine to anyone I choose. Now I will give your countries to King Nebuchadnezzar of Babylon, who is my servant. I have put everything, even the wild animals, under his control. All the nations will serve him, his son, and his grandson until his time is up. Then many nations and great kings will conquer and rule over Babylon. So you must submit to Babylon's king and serve him; put your neck under Babylon's yoke! I will punish any nation that refuses to be his slave, says the Lord. I will send war, famine, and disease upon that nation until Babylon has conquered it.

Jesus affirmed the symbolism of power, but He rejected the symbolism of worship of Caesar on the coin. The imperial tax was the way the people of God expressed their relationship to the empire. The people of God also paid a temple tax, which expressed their relationship to the kingdom of God. During Holy Week, Jesus submitted to the rule of Caesar but also to the dominion of God. He knew that His murder at Rome's hands would ultimately fulfill God's work.

4 BC—Herod died and was buried in the Herodium. After Herod's death, his three sons ruled for a brief period, but then the Romans took over. They imposed heavy taxes and ruled with insensitivity, which led to growing Jewish discontent.

AD 6/7—Judea became a Roman province and Jesus visited the temple as a boy.

AD 14—Tiberius Caesar succeeded Caesar Augustus as Roman emperor; he did not disturb the foundations laid by Augustus and ruled with restraint and tact. He was assassinated in AD 37.

AD 15—Pontius Pilate was appointed procurator of Judea. He hated the Jews and was in frequent conflict with them (Luke 13:1; Mark 15:7).

AD 18—Caiaphas became high priest, and Pilate came to Jerusalem.

Accounts document Pilate's bribery, arbitrary action, expropriations, torture, insults, countless illegal executions, and ruthless cruelty.

AD 26—John the Baptist began his ministry.

AD 28—Baptism of Jesus and beginning of His ministry; Augustus brought his message: "You are the people of the kingdom on earth," and he hoped the political structures he formed would last forever. Jesus's message spoke of a kingdom "not of this earth." Even though Jesus rode into Jerusalem on Palm Sunday as a powerless, earthly king, His kingdom has endured. Despite world domination by evil rulers, His kingdom has persisted and flourished, enabling men to experience God's grace, rather than or even in the midst of man's tyranny.

AD 30—Jesus was crucified, rose from the dead, and ascended into heaven; Pentecost and the early church began.

AD 35—Paul's conversion on the road to Damascus; Paul had attended the Torah School of Rabbi Gamaliel, son-in-law of Hillel (who had established Jewish understanding of the scriptures), in Jerusalem. Paul became a Pharisee. Pharisees took God's statutes seriously. They believed, as many Orthodox Jews do today, that if only one Sabbath could be kept without failure, then the Messiah would come. When Jesus offered the kingdom of God to sinners, He attacked their authority and, even worse, claimed He was the Messiah! When Paul was sent to Damascus to deal with Christians (whom he saw as Jewish apostates), Jesus appeared to him, which changed everything. The man who once persecuted Christians became the key evangelist to the Gentiles.

AD 37—Caligula became emperor of Roman Empire. He was murdered by soldiers in AD 41.

AD 40—Herod Agrippa was appointed king of Judea.

AD 41—Claudius became Roman emperor. He exiled the philosopher Seneca. Seneca later was brought back by Agrippina, Claudius's fourth wife, who made him a tutor of her son Nero. She had Claudius poisoned in AD 54 so Nero could reign.

AD 44—James was martyred, and Peter was imprisoned.

AD 46—Paul's first missionary journey.

AD 49/50—The Jerusalem Council.

AD 50–52—Paul's second missionary journey.

AD 53–57—Paul's third missionary journey.

AD 54—Nero became Roman emperor. Rome burned in AD 64, and Nero erected grand buildings in the vacant space, which ruined the imperial finances. He persecuted Christians; he covered them in tar and set them on fire as living torches in imperial parks, and women were shamelessly exhibited in mythological pantomimes before being devoured by wild beasts. Even the Roman mob was horrified. Nero committed suicide in AD 68 when the senate turned on him.

AD 57—Paul wrote the book of Romans and was imprisoned in Caesarea.

AD 59—Paul's voyage to Rome, where he was imprisoned until AD 62, during which time he wrote his "prison letters."

AD 66–73—First Jewish-Roman war.

AD 67/68—Paul was martyred by the sword outside the walls of Rome.

AD 68—Galba became Roman emperor. He was lynched by soldiers in AD 69.

AD 69—Vitellius became Roman emperor. He was lynched by soldiers eleven months later.

AD 69—Otho became Roman emperor. He committed suicide three months later.

AD 69—Vespasian became Roman emperor. He died of natural causes in AD 79.

AD 70—Romans destroyed Jerusalem. After the destruction of the temple, the Sicarii, an extremist Jewish splinter group, fled Jerusalem and settled in Masada after killing the Roman garrison there.

AD 73–960—Jews committed mass suicide at Masada while under siege and Roman attack.

AD 79—Titus became Roman emperor. He died a natural death in AD 81. Mount Vesuvius erupted on August 23, 79. The cities of Pompeii and Herculaneum were buried under ash.

AD 81—Domitian became Roman emperor. Pliny called Domitian the beast from hell. Domitian took emperor worship to a new level and called himself "God the Lord." He referred to his throne as the seat of the gods. He saw Christ as a figure within Christianity who competed with the Caesars for allegiance, which explained his persecution of Christians. He established the Capitoline Games and celebrated the traditional festivals of the seasons, processions, spectacles, games, and shows with unheard of extravagance.

The circus became a temple, and the people's festival became the worship of the emperor. The head of the Ephesian cult of the emperor was the high priest of Asia, who was also president of the government of Asia with the title of *asiarch*. A new temple was built in Ephesus with a statue of Domitian four times life-size. However, the senate hated Domitian because of his obsession with self-worship and cruelty. At the same time, the apostle John lived in Ephesus and opposed the worship of Domitian. History states John was brought to Rome, examined, tortured, and then banished to Patmos for his faith.

AD 95—Apostle John wrote the book of Revelation while on Patmos. Domitian prefigured the Antichrist to come. Domitian was murdered in AD 96. Ephesus became the center for persecution of Christianity. In Ephesus, Smyrna, Pergamon, and elsewhere, there were severe anti-Christian riots and executions.

AD 96—Nerva became Roman emperor. He died a natural death in 98.

AD 98—Trajan became Roman emperor. He died a natural death in 117.

AD 117—Hadrian became Roman emperor. He died a natural death in 138.

AD 132—Hadrian rebuilt Jerusalem as Aelia Capitolina, a Roman city that Jews were forbidden to enter.

AD 132–135—Second Jewish war, led by Simon Bar-Kokba, was crushed by the Romans. Jews were banned from Jerusalem and Judea. Many Jews were sold into slavery and sent to Rome. Jews fled; this was the Diaspora. There was no further occupation until the beginning of Jewish immigration in the nineteenth century. The Romans (70–324), Byzantines (324–638), Muslims (638–1099), Crusaders (1099–1187), Muslims (1187–1516), Turks (1516–1917), and the British (1917–1947) all successively laid claim to the territory in the city of David and in the land promised to Abraham and his descendants.

AD 138—Antoninus Pius became Roman emperor. He died a natural death in 161.

AD 161—Marcus Aurelius became Roman emperor. He was said to be the last of the "five good emperors." The historian Herodian wrote, "He gave proof of his learning not by mere words or knowledge of philosophical doctrines but by his blameless character and temperate way of life." He spoke of the Christians as "men who knew how to die." He died of the plague in 180.

AD 180—Commodus became Roman emperor. He was murdered by courtiers in 192.

AD 160–225—Tertullian was the founder of Western theology and a Christian apologist. He represented a view that may seem foreign to many today in that he saw the empire of the Caesars as the forerunner to the empire of Christ. Hence, Christians were to intercede to God on behalf of the empire. He wrote, "The truth knows that it has no home on earth, and is a stranger in a hostile world, and that its origin, its home, its hope, its validity and its future are in heaven."

AD 250—Emperor Decius issued Decius's edict of persecution. The edict required Christians to participate in state sacrifices and reject their faith. In the face of this first systematic persecution, many Christians chose to die rather than deny their faith in Christ. The edict lasted seventeen months. Then Decius ended the persecutions.

AD 258—Emperor Valerian issued his edict of persecution. His son suspended the edict after four years.

AD 284—Diocletian became emperor. He also issued an edict of persecution. Christians were bound, packed in cargo boats, and sent out to simply drift on the sea. In Asia Minor, the persecution became almost a military operation. Armed legions surrounded towns and hunted down the Christians.

Second and third century AD—Jewish religious schools became active in Galilee, and academics wrote down Jewish oral law with commentaries that became the Talmud.

306—Constantine became emperor. He moved the capital from Rome to Byzantium (renamed Constantinople). His mother, Helena, went on a pilgrimage to Jerusalem.

311—Constantine's edict of tolerance granted freedom of worship to Christians, and in 313, Constantine's first coin was minted with a tiny cross of Christ on it. It symbolized that the war against Christianity was finally over after three hundred years.

313—Edict of Milan; Christianity was made a legal religion in the Roman Empire. Instead of seeing himself as divine, Constantine believed the emperor was installed by God and was perpetrated by God's grace, hence the term *Instinctu Divinitatis,* or "impelled by God."

315—Constantine struck coins with the monogram of Christ's name and cross/scepter. Constantine saw his earthly kingdom as a prefiguration of Christ's kingdom, which, when it comes, will make an end to Satan and evil forever.

325—Council of Nicaea; Constantine assembled church fathers to celebrate the twentieth anniversary of his reign.

326—Founding of Constantinople; Constantine struck a coin bearing his standard with the monogram of the name of Christ triumphantly raised above a pierced snake. He saw himself as the warrior for Christ against the forces of hell.

335—Church of the Holy Sepulchre was dedicated in Jerusalem.

379–395—Reign of Theodosius; Christianity became the official state religion.

395—The Roman Empire was divided into the east (Greek-speaking) and west (Latin-speaking). The west fell to Germanic invaders, but the Byzantium Empire survived. Churches and monasteries were built.

614—Persian army was massacred by Christians, who desecrated their holy sites.

628—The Prophet Mohammad conquered Mecca. The Persians were driven out by the Byzantium Empire.

638—Omar (Mohammad's successor) defeated the Byzantines at the Yarmuk River in Syria.

691—The Islamic shrine the Dome of the Rock was completed, as was the El-Aqsa mosque (*Hara mesh-Sharif,* or "sacred precinct"). Christians were allowed safe passage to the Holy Land until 1009, when the third Fatimid caliph, El-Hakim, initiated violent persecution of non-Muslims and destroyed the Holy Sepulchre.

1071—Jerusalem fell to the Seljuk Turks, who forbade Christians access to the Holy City. Christian Europe was outraged, which led to a series of Crusades over the next two hundred years to take back Jerusalem and the biblical sites in Palestine.

1099—First crusade; crusaders took Jerusalem with a massive slaughter in the streets.

1119—Founding of the Knights Templar, a military order of monastic knights, headquartered in the temple area of Jerusalem.

1148—Second crusade; the army was defeated while besieging Damascus.

1187—Saladin defeated the crusaders at the Horns of Haltin and took Jerusalem.

1188–1192—The third crusade reconquered much of the coast. Richard I (Richard the Lionheart) failed to take Jerusalem but negotiated the right of access for pilgrims.

1260—Mamelukes (former slave guards of Saladin's Ayyubid dynasty) defeated the invading Mongols. Baybars became sultan of Egypt.

1291—The last Latin strongholds in the Holy Land fell to Mamelukes. Christian knights were driven from the Holy Land, but Christian pilgrims were allowed.

1453—Ottoman Turks captured Constantinople and renamed it Istanbul.

1492—Spanish Inquisition; King Ferdinand expelled all professing Jews and Muslims from Spain. The Jews started returning to Palestine.

1516—Ottoman Turks defeated the Mamelukes and seized control of Palestine and Egypt.

1520–1566—Suleyman the Magnificent (the Ottomans' greatest sultan) built vast architectural projects in Jerusalem, especially the city walls and gates.

1831—Muhammad Ali, Egyptian ruler, seized Palestine, but with British help the Turks regained control. Jewish immigration continued due to anti-Semitism and pogroms in eastern Europe and the Russian Empire.

1860—Jerusalem's first Jewish settlements since the Diaspora.

1882—Jewish census indicated twenty-four thousand Jewish residents lived in Palestine.

1897—World Zionist Organization formed, with Theodor Herzl as head, "to create for the Jewish people a home in Palestine." He convened the First Zionist Congress in Basel, Switzerland, to establish a safe place for Jewish people to live. The national flag was selected, taken from the blue and white of the prayer shawl (*tallith*), and the national anthem was chosen, "Hatikvah" (the Hope). A Jewish national bank and a land bank were created which began buying land.

Nov. 2, 1917—The Balfour Declaration was issued by Great Britain. It favored the establishment of a national home for the Jewish people in Palestine. Later that month, Sir Edmund Allenby led the charge that gave Great Britain control over Jerusalem. As he entered the Jaffa Gate, he dismounted his horse and took off his hat, believing that none other than the Messiah should enter Jerusalem mounted on a steed. The Jewish population had increased to eighty-five thousand.

1920—Following World War I, the League of Nations gave Britain control of Palestine, but the Balfour Declaration was forgotten. The British feared Arab retribution and turned against Jewish immigration by decreasing the quotas for returning Jews. They installed an Arab government and sent illegal immigrants either back to their city of origin or to detention camps on Cyprus.

1923—The British recognized Trans-Jordan as an autonomous Arab emirate ruled by Emir Abdullah, with Amman as the capital.

1936—Arabs revolted in Palestine due to Jews returning.

1937—The Peel Commission proposed the partitioning of Palestine. Jews accepted, but the Arabs refused.

1939—The British limited Jewish immigration, but Jews continued to arrive due to Nazism. Jewish population had increased to 335,000.

November 1947—United Nations voted to permit the establishment of the modern state of Israel in May 1948 (fulfilling Isaiah 66:8). The Jewish population then numbered just less than one million.

May 14, 1948—David Ben Gurion declared the birth of the state of Israel. The War of Independence; when Israel was granted a certain land allotment for the state, the surrounding Arab nations did not honor the resolution and immediately went to war.

December 1949—Armistice signed. As a result of the war, Israel gained significant territory. More than half a million Arabs were made refugees in neighboring Arab countries, Gaza Strip (controlled by Egypt), and Jordanian-held territories on the West Bank of the Jordan River. Jerusalem's control was divided. Israel passed the Law of Return, which extended to all Jews worldwide.

1956—Suez Crisis or the Second Arab–Israeli War; Israel invaded Egypt in late 1956, followed by the United Kingdom and France, in order to regain control of the Suez Canal. The canal did not reopen until March 1957.

June 1967—The Six-Day War; Egypt built up forces at the border, which alarmed Israel, so Israel made a preemptive strike. Israel held off six invading Arab nations and recaptured the city of Jerusalem. This was the first sovereign possession of the city since 586 BC, when the last Jewish king in David's lineage was driven from the city. Israel captured the Golan Heights from Syria, Gaza Strip and Sinai from Egypt, the West Bank from Jordan, and all Jerusalem.

October 6, 1973—Yom Kippur War; Israel held back an Egyptian-Syrian invasion and captured more land.

1979—Camp David Agreement; Egypt and Israel signed a peace treaty.

1982—Israel returned Sinai to Egypt.

1987–1993—First Intifada ("shaking off"), a grass roots Palestinian revolt against Israel's occupation in the Gaza Strip and West Bank.

1993—Oslo Accords between Israel and PLO.

1994— Israel and Jordan formally ended the state of war; Palestinians were granted limited autonomy.

2000—In the fifty years of Israel's history, her people had returned from over one hundred nations. The population of Jews was six million. Ezekiel spoke of a time when the Jews would all gather to their own land, "not leaving any behind" (Ezekiel 39:28).

September 2000–February 8, 2005—Second Intifada; the second Palestinian uprising began after Ariel Sharon made a visit to the Temple Mount. Nearly a thousand Israelis and over three thousand Palestinians lost their lives due to the fighting.

2005—Israel withdrew its Jewish settlement from Gaza.

October 2005—Iran's president Mahmoud Ahmadinejad quoted Ayatollah Ruhollah Khomeini, the founder of the Islamic Republic of Iran, in an address to the World without Zionism conference in Teheran, calling for the destruction of Israel.

2006—The Lebanon War; this was precipitated by Hezbollah militants firing rockets at Israeli border towns. Israel countered with Operation Just Reward.

2008—Census indicated a population of 7,465,500 inhabitants in Israel (75.5 percent, or 5,634,300, were Jewish).

2009—The Tamar Gas Field was discovered in the Mediterranean Sea off the coast of Israel.

PART 2
The Geography of the Bible

Two maps are included in this section. Map 1 shows the Middle East in Old Testament times, and map 2 shows Israel in New Testament times.

God made a covenant with Abraham to give his descendants, the children of Israel, the Promised Land, a land flowing with milk and honey (i.e., a prosperous land). In order for any land to be prosperous, several things are necessary. First, you need water because without water you can't raise animals, and you can't grow crops. Second, you need roads for transportation.

The Fertile Crescent was named as such because it represents the lands encompassed by a crescent shape that extends from Egypt in the south to the north through Israel and up into Lebanon and Turkey, and then it extends southeast into Mesopotamia. These lands were fertile and heavily populated because of their access to water, which included the Nile River in Egypt and the Euphrates and Tigris Rivers in Mesopotamia. Today, the Fertile Crescent includes the countries of Egypt, Israel, Palestine, Jordan, Lebanon, Southeastern Turkey, Cyprus, and Syria; the western parts of Iran and Iraq are also included in the Fertile Crescent. Water also meant the possibility of agriculture, which was necessary to support larger populations. Larger populations led to larger military forces, which unfortunately led to expansionist political policies.

If you look at map 1, you will easily recognize that Israel is a bridge between Egypt in the south and the other lands of the Fertile Crescent to the north and east. Canaan was seen as the gateway to Egypt, and therefore its rulers kept a presence there. The two ancient centers of the world, often in conflict, included Egypt versus the armies of Mesopotamia (Assyria,

Babylonia, and later Medo-Persia). Since Israel was the land bridge between the two, it was often caught in the conflicts. Armies not uncommonly destroyed everything in their paths. This resulted in the destruction of the kingdom of Israel (the northern kingdom, also called Samaria) by the Assyrians during the Assyrian-Egyptian war and the subsequent destruction of the kingdom of Judah (the southern kingdom) during the Babylonian-Egyptian war.

The two main highways that ran north and south were the Sea Highway (Via Maris, which means the way of the sea), which paralleled the Mediterranean coast in Israel, and the King's Highway that ran just east of the mountain range on the plateau that ran from the Arabian Sea through the lands of Edom, Moab, Ammon, Gilead, Bashan (Golan Heights), and then on to Damascus in Syria. These five areas were separated from south to north by the Zered, Arnon, Jabbok, and Yarmuk Rivers, respectively. The Sea Highway ran through cultivated lands with water sources, and the King's Highway ran alongside desert terrain. It was much easier for armies and trading caravans to travel from Mesopotamia to Egypt or vice versa by land, rather than navigate the difficult currents and tides of the sea (which were impassable six months out of the year during winter). These two highways were connected by a number of east/west roads, but traveling was difficult due to valleys and hills. Jerusalem, the capital of Israel, was midway between these two highways, and this made paved roads essential, connecting Jerusalem to both of them (today this is Interstate 1, which goes from Tel Aviv to Jerusalem and then east into Jordan). In biblical times, the coastal areas were heavily forested and contained swamps, making passage difficult. This made the roads all the more essential.

Another important road was called the Way of the Patriarchs, named so because most of Abraham's, most of Isaac's, and some of Jacob's travels were along this road, which ran in the hill country and avoided the Canaanites, who lived in the lowlands. It began in the Beer Sheba Valley in the south and ran north to Hebron and all the way to Jezreel (current Highway 60). Although relations between herdsmen and farmers often were tense, both needed each other. The herdsmen needed grain, fruit, and vegetables provided by city dwellers. They also needed weapons and pottery. The city dwellers needed milk, meat, and hides from the herdsmen. The nomadic herdsmen were susceptible to droughts and famine, which, as we will see, led to Abraham and Jacob both traveling to Egypt in order to survive.

Not only was Israel a land of strategic importance, but it was the point where the continents of Africa, Asia, and Europe met.

The country of Israel has a variety of weather conditions due to its diverse geography, which includes the coastal area along the Mediterranean (Great) Sea, the mountains in the east, the agricultural lands in between, the desert land of the Negev, and the Dead (Salt) Sea, the lowest location on the earth. Settlements have always depended upon the spring and fall rains and the water that flows down from the mountain areas. The rainy season begins in October and lasts until April. The rain runs down from the mountains in the north into the Jordan River, which feeds into the Sea of Galilee (Sea of Kinneret, Sea of Tiberias), into the Mediterranean Sea, or into the Jordan Valley to the Dead Sea. Mountain dwellers dug cisterns and pools to collect rainwater. The rock formation in the hills is chalky, which holds water; it was used to plaster the walls of cisterns. Fortunately, Israel has many springs scattered throughout the country.

Although not particularly rich in natural resources, asphalt and salt were exported to Egypt from the Dead Sea, copper was mined at Timna, and iron ore also was mined from the Mountains of Gilead.

At the time of Christ (see map 2), the Romans exploited Israel in order to spread their culture. The Decapolis (a Greek term meaning "ten cities"), especially Scythopolis (Beth Shean), was the chief way Roman life spread to the east. Subsequently, the land was important to the spread of Christianity for the same reason, as it was the boundary between Christian and pagan worlds.

Without a basic understanding of the geography of Israel, it is difficult to appreciate how the land was initially settled by the Israelites. Early on, the Israelites were the mountain dwellers, and the Canaanites were the lowland dwellers. The former were nomadic herdsmen, and the latter were agronomists (farmers) with some urban communities. The religion and culture of the Israelites were completely different from that of the Canaanites. It was not until the period of Israel's kings that the Israelites moved into the lowlands.

Map 1

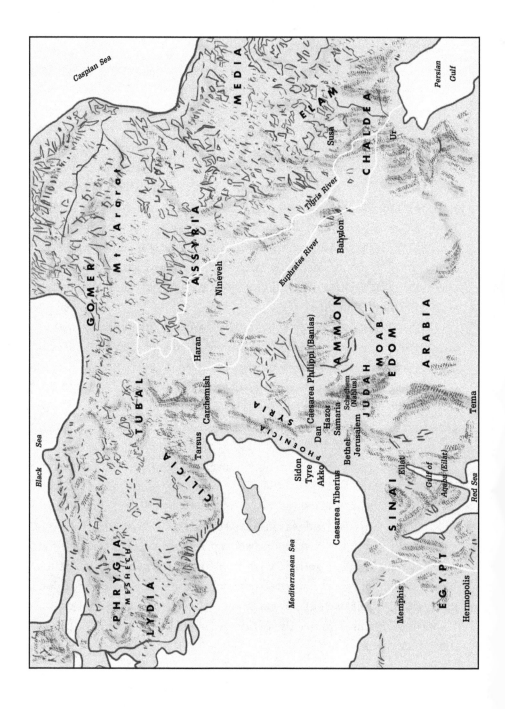

Map 2

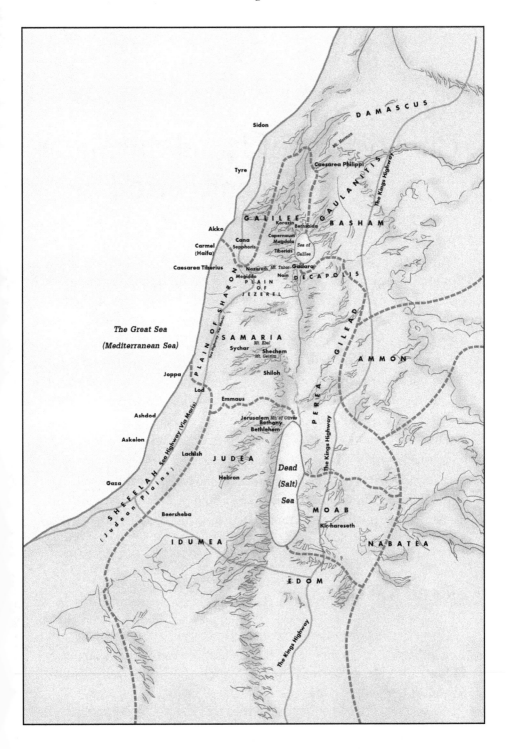

PART 3
The History of Israel during the Old Testament Period

The majority of the prophecies in the Bible concern the children of Israel. Now that we have a basic understanding of the geography of the Promised Land, we can turn to its history. The history of Israel is given in the Old Testament; I will start at the beginning and go book by book, giving a brief overview.

The first messianic prophecy is recorded in Genesis 3. It was given to Adam and Eve after they sinned. God created man and gave him control of the earth, and he was to rule over it (Genesis 1:28). But when man rebelled against God and sinned in the fall, humanity essentially transferred its authority to Satan. God issued a death sentence to Satan and said he would be crushed by the "seed" of a woman (Genesis 3:15). Genealogies were normally given through the descendants of the male, not the female. But as you will see, the scriptures state Jesus would be born of a virgin. This happened when the Holy Spirit came upon Mary to fertilize her seed. Hence, Jesus was born both the Son of Man and the Son of God.

2166 BC—Abram

Prophecy concerning the nation of Israel really started with Abram around 2166 BC. Abram's father was Terah. He lived with his family in a place called Ur of the Chaldeans, which was about one hundred miles northwest of the Persian Gulf on the Euphrates River. Terah moved with his family heading for the land of Canaan, but they settled in Haran, which was located in present-day Turkey. Terah died in Haran. Sometime later, God spoke to Abram and told him to leave Haran and go to a place that God would show him. God prophetically made a promise to Abram:

> Now the Lord had said unto Abram, "Get thee out of thy country, and from thy kindred, and from thy father's house, unto a land that I will shew thee: And I will make of thee a great nation, and I will bless thee, and make thy name great; and thou shalt be a blessing: And I will bless them that bless thee, and curse him that curseth thee: and in thee shall all families of the earth be blessed." (Genesis 12:1–3)

Imagine God showing up one day and telling you to leave the country where you had grown up and to leave all of your relatives. That's the downside. Then He goes on to promise He will lead you to a new land where He will bless you so much that you'll go on to become famous and have so many descendants that you will become a great nation. But God doesn't stop there. He then promises that whoever helps you, He will help, but whoever does evil toward you, He will punish. God also says that through your descendants all the "families of the earth" are going to be blessed. This subsequently would occur in a variety of ways, but the most important way was when Jesus came as the Savior of the whole world, fulfilling this promise. Jesus's ministry on the earth was to His own people, the Jews (Matthew 15:24). However, His death and resurrection were for all people.

God established an amazing relationship with Abram. Abram must have been convinced of what God told him because he did exactly what God had commanded him.

2091 BC—Abraham Enters Canaan

At age seventy-five, Abram left Haran with his wife, Sarai, his nephew Lot, and all of his household, and they traveled to Canaan. In Genesis 12:7, God told Abram, "And the Lord appeared unto Abram, and said, 'Unto thy seed will I give this land: and there builded he an altar unto the Lord, who appeared unto him.'" We're not told exactly what kind of map or GPS system God used to lead Abram to Canaan, but nonetheless, he arrived.

Sometime after that, God spoke to Abram in a vision and promised him a son, even though he and his wife were very old and beyond childbearing age. Abram questioned God, asking Him how he could be sure this would happen. Genesis 15 records what happened next:

> As the sun was setting, Abram fell into a deep sleep, and a thick and dreadful darkness came over him. Then the Lord said to him, "Know for certain that for four hundred years your descendants will be strangers in a country not their own and that they will be enslaved and mistreated there. But I will punish the nation they serve as slaves, and afterward they will come out with great possessions. You, however, will go to your ancestors in peace and be buried at a good old age. In the fourth generation your descendants will come back here, for the sin of the Amorites has not yet reached its full measure." When the sun had set and darkness had fallen, a smoking firepot with a blazing torch appeared and passed between the pieces. On that day the Lord made a covenant with Abram and said, "To your descendants I give this land, from the Wadi of Egypt to the great river, the Euphrates—the land of the Kenites, Kenizzites, Kadmonites, Hittites, Perizzites, Rephaites, Amorites, Canaanites, Girgashites and Jebusites." (Genesis 15:12–21 NIV)

What happened here is that God made a blood covenant with Abram. Blood covenants seem strange to us today, but they were common in the East at that time. Usually the blood covenant was bilateral, and after the animals were cut in two and the pieces laid side by side, each person walked between the pieces, essentially saying, "If I break this covenant, do to me what we have done to these animals." Pretty graphic! I suspect if we made our wedding vows today in a similar manner, we would see a lot less divorce. This covenant, however, was not bilateral but unilateral. It did not depend on what Abram did. God simply told Abram what He planned to do. There were a number of prophetic promises here:

- God predicted Abram's descendants, the Hebrews, would be enslaved for four hundred years. This predicted the Egyptian captivity.
- God promised the people would leave Egypt with great wealth. This predicted the Exodus.
- God told Abram he would die peacefully, which he did.
- God named all the lands that Abram's descendants would receive.

Sometimes it's difficult to wait on God to do what He's promised. This happened with Abram's wife, Sarai. She so desperately wanted a child that she convinced Abram to take her Egyptian servant Hagar to be his wife also and have children by her. Abram did this, and Hagar became pregnant. Hagar then began to show contempt for Sarai. Sarai spoke harshly to her, and Hagar ran away. At a spring in the wilderness, an angel appeared to Hagar and spoke to her.

> And the angel of the Lord said unto her, "Return to thy mistress, and submit thyself under her hands." And the angel of the Lord said unto her, "I will multiply thy seed exceedingly, that it shall not be numbered for multitude." And the angel of the Lord said unto her, "Behold, thou art with child and shalt bear a son, and shalt call his name Ishmael; because the Lord hath heard thy affliction. And he will be a wild man; his hand will be against every man, and every man's hand against him; and he shall dwell in the presence of all his brethren." (Genesis 16:9–12)

God told Hagar to go back to Abram's house and tolerate Sarai's abuse. God promised that if she obeyed, her son Ishmael would become a nation with many descendants. Ishmael did indeed become the father of all the Arabic peoples. This meant that the Jews and Arabs were half brothers; the conflict between them has persisted to this day. Repeated conflicts have occurred in recent times, ever since the state of Israel was established in

1948. Immediately thereafter, Israel was attacked by the surrounding Arab nations in the War of Independence. Then there was the Six-Day War of 1967 and the War of Yom Kippur in 1973. Just look at the consequences when Abram took his wife's advice, and they chose to have children by a different route than God's intended plan.

When Abram was ninety-nine years old, God appeared to him once again and said He was going to make a covenant with Abram. God again promised that Abram would have many descendants, and they would become a great nation. God changed Abram's name to Abraham and Sarai's name to Sarah. Names were very significant in ancient times. The name Abram means "exalted father," and Abraham probably means "father of many." Sarai and Sarah both mean "princess." God told Abraham that the land of Canaan would become the "everlasting possession" of his descendants. But now God required something new from Abraham, namely circumcision.

Circumcision would be required of all males as a covenant mark, showing they were God's people. Abraham's part in the covenant was to circumcise every male at eight days of age. Then God told him Sarah was going to have a child. Abraham laughed at the idea of having a son at age one hundred. So God told him to name his son *Isaac*, which means "he laughs." Here God was reconfirming and extending the covenant He previously made with him. Abraham also asked for a blessing for his son Ishmael, and God told him that he also would become a great nation.

Read Genesis 17:1–21.

The word circumcision comes from the Latin word *circumcidere*, which means "to cut around." The whole idea of circumcision makes men nervous for obvious reasons. The big question is, "What's the big deal about a little piece of skin, especially a piece in that area?" Circumcision has been practiced by many nations for millennia. Currently, it is estimated that about one-third of the world's male population has been circumcised. For religious purposes, virtually all Jewish and Muslim men are circumcised. Circumcision is also practiced in the United States and parts of southern Africa and Asia. The procedure helps to prevent the spread of some sexually transmitted diseases, especially HIV.

But God intended circumcision to be a physical demonstration of a spiritual truth or principle. It was not to be just an outward mark to identify

His chosen people; it was to be inward as well. The cutting away of the flesh was the covenant mark of what occurred internally, indicating one's covenantal relationship and commitment to God. The apostle Paul pointed this out.

> For you are not a true Jew just because you were born of Jewish parents or because you have gone through the ceremony of circumcision. No, a true Jew is one whose heart is right with God. And true circumcision is not merely obeying the letter of the law; rather, it is a change of heart produced by the Spirit. And a person with a changed heart seeks praise from God, not from people. (Romans 2:28–29 NLT)

As one would expect, both Abraham and Sarah were having a hard time buying into this idea of having a son at their ages, but nonetheless, just as God had promised, Isaac arrived a year later. I wonder what it was like for Sarah when she started showing signs of pregnancy—bulging and gaining weight. At first she probably thought, *I really need to cut back on all these carbs!* But as she got bigger, she must have wondered, *Could this really be happening?* Then, when quickening occurred—when she first felt Isaac move within her womb—she must have been overjoyed. I can just see God smiling all the while! What a faith-booster that entire experience must have been for Abraham and Sarah.

2066 BC—The Birth of Isaac

Let me return to the specifics of this covenant. First of all, this covenant was bilateral. If Abraham did his part, God promised to do His part, which included the following:

- God would greatly increase the people, and Abraham would be the father of many nations.
- God promised Abraham prosperity.
- God promised that this would be an *everlasting covenant* with Abraham's descendants, and He would be their God *forever.*

- God initiated the *covenant of circumcision* as an identifying mark to show they were His people.
- God promised a son, Isaac.
- God also promised to bless Ishmael and his descendants and make them into a great nation.

Next, in Genesis 22 we find that God made a strange request of Abraham in order to test his faith. He instructed Abraham to take Isaac and sacrifice him. Pagan nations practiced human sacrifice, but God condemned it as a terrible sin (Leviticus 20:1–5). God, however, never intended for Isaac to die. He was testing Abraham's loyalty. In obedience, Abraham took Isaac to Mount Moriah (the Temple Mount area in Jerusalem today) and prepared to sacrifice him. Just as he was about to slay his only son, God called out to Abraham and stopped him. Abraham saw a ram stuck in the bushes and sacrificed it in place of Isaac. Because Abraham had demonstrated his faith, God promised to make his descendants "as numerous as the stars," and they would conquer their enemies' cities. God also repeated the promise of Genesis 12 that all the nations of the earth would be blessed by them.

Read Genesis 28:11–22.

2006 BC—The Birth of Jacob and Esau

Isaac grew up and married a woman named Rebekah. Abraham died at age 175. Rebekah became pregnant and gave birth to twins, Esau and Jacob. Esau was born first and deserved the birthright (the rights of a firstborn) from his father, but Rebekah conspired with Jacob, and they tricked Isaac. Isaac was almost blind, so when Jacob came to him, claiming to be Esau, Isaac gave Jacob the birthright blessing. This plot, however, had its consequences because after that, Esau hated Jacob and even wanted to kill him. The descendants of Esau were the Edomites, and they were always antagonistic to their cousins the Israelites. They often supported other nations who fought against the Israelites. Because of this, the prophets Isaiah, Joel, Amos, Obadiah, and Ezekiel all prophesied Edom's judgment and destruction. Where are the ancient cities of Edom today? As I will show, they don't exist!

Rebekah heard of Esau's plan to kill Jacob and told Jacob to flee to her brother Laban in Haran, which he did. As he traveled, he had a dream. In the dream, Jacob saw a ladder from the earth to heaven, with angels going up and down. He also saw God in heaven, who told Jacob He was going to give him the land where he was lying. And through the dream, God went on to reconfirm the covenant He had previously made with Abraham. God promised to watch over Jacob and give him many descendants and that his descendants would bless "all the peoples of the earth." When Jacob awoke, he took the stone he had used for a pillow and dedicated it and the place to God. He called the place *Bethel*. Jacob made a vow to God, basically saying that if God took care of him and eventually brought him back home to his father's house, he would tithe a tenth of everything to God.

Read Genesis 28:11–22.

When the King James Version of the Bible was translated in 1611, the word *tithe* was understood to mean a tenth of one's income. It is interesting that Jacob made his tithe conditional. He promised to tithe *if* God would be with him and protect him. Notice the connection between faithfully tithing to God and God's faithfulness of protection and providence. The Bible makes it clear that everything belongs to God (Exodus 19:5; Deuteronomy 10:14; Job 41:11; Psalm 24:1; 1 Corinthians 10:26). Jesus was asked if taxes should be paid to the government. He responded that we should not only pay our taxes to the government, but we also should pay our tithe to God (Mark 12:13–17). Hence, we owe our taxes to the government for what it does for us. We also owe our tithes to God for what He has given and has done for us. The fact that we earn our money does not exempt us from paying taxes, nor does it exempt us from paying our tithes. In other words, our tithes are not optional, as many people believe. In fact, the prophet Malachi stated that not paying our tithes is robbing God (Malachi 3:7–8). Have you ever thought that not paying your tithe is tantamount to stealing from God? Well, God sees it that way. That may seem like a bummer, but you not only are stealing from God but also are robbing yourself of God's protection and providence.

Many scriptures link tithing and God's provision. Malachi 3:10 states, "Bring ye all the tithes into the storehouse, that there may be meat in mine house, and prove me now herewith, saith the Lord of hosts, if I will not open you the windows of heaven, and pour you out a blessing, that there shall not be room enough to receive it." Similarly, Solomon stated in Proverbs 3:9–10, "Honour the Lord with thy substance, and with the firstfruits of all thine increase: So shall thy barns be filled with plenty, and thy presses shall burst out with new wine."

Those scripture verses seem clear about the connection of tithing and blessing, but I am not preaching the prosperity gospel of "Name it, and claim it" here. Tithing is not just about our money; it's about our entire lives. Moses made it quite clear that God's blessing was linked to our behavior; that is, our obedience to God's laws (Deuteronomy 12:28). You can't write a big fat check to your church and then go out and commit adultery and expect God to bless you. It doesn't work that way. Jesus summed it up in Matthew 6:33 when He stated, "But seek ye first the kingdom of God, and his righteousness; and all these things shall be added unto you."

1929 BC—Jacob Flees to Haran

Jacob traveled on to his uncle Laban's home and wanted to a marry his daughter Rachel. Laban agreed—if Jacob would work seven years for him, which Jacob did. Following the wedding night, however, Jacob realized Laban had deceived him, and he had married Rachel's sister Leah, rather than Rachel. Jacob asked, "What have you done?" Laban made the excuse that the older daughter had to marry first. He promised Jacob he also could marry Rachel if he worked another seven years, which he did. In the end, Jacob also married Zilpah, Leah's servant, and Bilhah, Rachel's servant. This led to Jacob's thirteen children (twelve sons and one daughter).

- Zilpah bore Gad and Asher.
- Leah bore Reuben, Simeon, Levi, Judah, Issachar, Zebulun, and Dinah (the only daughter).
- Rachel bore Joseph and Benjamin.
- Bilhah bore Dan and Naphtali.

A common question that arises is the issue of polygamy. From the very beginning, God intended that marriage would be a covenantal relationship between one man and one woman, and they would remain together, separated only by death. In Genesis 2:24, God stated that the man and woman should "cleave" to each other and become "one flesh." The sacredness of marriage is affirmed in the Bible when it compares the marriage relationship to the relationship of Christ and the church (Ephesians 5:23–33).

Of their own accord, men began to take more than one wife. God seemed to tolerate this behavior, but there were many adverse consequences to polygamy. We saw what the jealousy between Sarah and Hagar led to. Similarly, God instructed the kings of Israel not to take many wives (Deuteronomy 17:17), but Solomon did not listen and took hundreds of wives. The wives eventually turned his heart away from God and led to idolatry, with bitter consequences. God regulated both divorce and polygamy in the laws of Moses, but the Bible never states He approved of them. In the New Testament, when the apostle Paul gave instructions to Timothy (1 Timothy 3:2, 12) and Titus (Titus 1:6) regarding leaders in the church, they were permitted to have only one wife.

Eventually, Jacob decided to return home with his entire family and household, but he was fearful of meeting his brother Esau and hoped to appease him by sending gifts on ahead. The night before Jacob met up with Esau, the Bible records that Jacob wrestled with God. Some theologians believe this was an Old Testament appearance of the preincarnate Christ. We know this was God, as Hosea 12:3 identified this being as God. God got Jacob alone, and they wrestled all night. As dawn was approaching, God touched Jacob's hip, injuring it, but Jacob still did not let go. God asked Jacob what his name was.

Now, two things are clear at this point. First, Jacob only lasted this long in the fight because God allowed him to do so. God could have easily ended it at any point. Second, when Jacob was asked what his name was, he probably didn't want to admit his name was Jacob, which means "the deceiver," but that was the truth! He had deceived his own brother and stolen his birthright. Jacob demanded that God bless him. God not only blessed him but changed his name to Israel. The name *Israel* means "God fights" or "God rules." I once heard a sermon titled "Going from Ordinary to Extraordinary!" Well, that is certainly what happened to Jacob that night. He held on to God with all his might and came away with an incredible blessing. He must have thought, *I am no longer Jacob, the deceiver, but Israel— God rules!*

Read Genesis 32:22–32.

Fortunately for Jacob, when he finally met Esau, Esau ran to him and embraced him.

God subsequently told Jacob to move to Bethel. At Bethel, God appeared to him again and blessed him once more, confirming his name as Israel. God also reconfirmed to Jacob, as He had done previously with Abraham and Isaac, that God was giving him the Promised Land. It was Jacob who gave the name of the place Bethel, which means "house of God."

Read Genesis 35:9–15.

One recurring theme throughout the Bible is that the Jews are inextricably linked to the land of Israel. As we will see, many nations will overrun and conquer Israel due to their sin of idolatry, but following periods of discipline, God always brings the Jews back.

Rachel died giving birth to Benjamin. Genesis 36 gives an account of Esau's descendants, the Edomites, who lived in the hill country of Seir (south and east of the Dead Sea). As I pointed out, the Edomites and Israelites always seemed to be at odds.

1898 BC—Joseph Is Sold into Slavery

Joseph was Jacob's favorite son, and his brothers resented it. They sold Joseph into slavery to Ishmaelite traders, who took him to Egypt. His brothers then covered his coat of many colors with animal blood to make Jacob think that Joseph had died from a wild animal attack.

While in Egypt, God watched out for Joseph. First he worked for Potiphar, the captain of the guard for Pharaoh. However, Potiphar's wife tried to proposition him, and he ran off. Potiphar's wife lied to her husband, accusing Joseph of coming on to her. So Potiphar had Joseph thrown into jail, where he got to know Pharaoh's chief cup-bearer and chief baker, who also were imprisoned. Subsequently, they each had a dream. Joseph interpreted the meaning of their dreams, and his interpretations came true.

1885 BC—Joseph Rules Egypt

Two years later, Pharaoh had a dream. While standing on the bank of the Nile River, he saw seven fat, healthy cows come up out of the river, followed by seven scrawny, thin cows. Then the scrawny cows ate the fat cows. Following this first dream, he had a second dream in which he saw seven heads of plump grain on a single stalk, followed by seven shriveled and withered heads. The thin heads then swallowed the plump heads. Pharaoh had no idea what the dreams meant, nor did his wise men. The king's chief cup-bearer, who had been restored to his position, remembered how Joseph had interpreted their dreams in prison. So Pharaoh sent for Joseph. Joseph told him his two dreams both meant the same thing. They were meant as a warning to Pharaoh, as there were going to be seven years of plentiful harvests followed by seven years of famine. Pharaoh was impressed and put Joseph, at age thirty, in charge of Egypt to prepare for the seven years of famine.

Read Genesis 41:41–46.

God had showed Joseph there were seven good years followed by seven years of famine. The famine also affected the land of Israel, so Jacob sent Joseph's ten older brothers down to Egypt to buy grain. When they met Joseph, he recognized them, but they didn't know who he was. I suspect by that time Joseph looked quite the part and spoke Egyptian. Joseph got them to bring their youngest brother Benjamin down with them on a subsequent trip. Eventually, Joseph revealed his identity to his brothers, who were stunned. Joseph told them something quite amazing. He told his brothers not to be angry with themselves or to grieve for what they had done to him because he realized that God actually had sent him to Egypt to preserve his family. Wow! He could have brought the hammer down on them. Instead, he demonstrated incredible maturity and wisdom. He saw how God had used their evil behavior to save their whole family. What amazes me most is that he did not appear to harbor any resentment.

Read Genesis 45:4–8.

There is a very important principle here. God is the Creator. He loves to create. That is who He is and what He does. In this situation, Jacob's brothers intended evil for Joseph, but ultimately, God used it for good. I believe that God loves to use the evil that Satan intends for us by flipping it (creating it) for our good. However, we have to behave like Joseph did, accepting the evil done to us and praising God in the midst of it, recognizing that nothing can happen to us unless God allows it. And if He allows it, then He will be faithful to use it for our good. (See Romans 8:28–29.)

At Joseph's request, Jacob's family moved to Egypt. On the way to Egypt, God spoke to Jacob one night, saying, "I am God, the God of thy father: fear not to go down into Egypt; for I will there make of thee a great nation: I will go down with thee into Egypt; and I will also surely bring thee up again: and Joseph shall put his hand upon thine eyes" (Genesis 46:3–4).

Imagine what that must have been like for Jacob. He finds out his favorite son is not only alive but second in command of all Egypt. However, he also finds out what Joseph's brothers had done to him. I wonder how they explained that to their father.

Pharaoh gave Jacob and his family excellent land in the region of Goshen, and they prospered in the land.

1805 BC—Joseph Dies

At the age of 147, Jacob called his sons in to tell them what would happen to them in the future. With regard to Judah, he blessed him and gave him the leadership position in the family that normally was associated with the firstborn son. Hence, he was to become the new head or patriarch of the family, and he was to receive twice the inheritance share as compared to his siblings. As part of the blessing, Jacob told Judah, "The scepter will not depart from Judah, nor the ruler's staff from his descendants, until the coming of the one to whom it belongs, the one whom all the nations will honor" (Genesis 49:10 NLT).

From the time of King David until Jesus came, the scepter literally did "not depart from Judah." Someone from the tribe of Judah always ruled. The phrase "until the coming of the one to whom it belongs" is traditionally rendered as "until Shiloh comes." Shiloh means "He whose right it is," and it is an ancient title of the Messiah. Over a millennium and a half later, Jesus did come. In Revelation, He is referred to as "the Lion of the tribe of Judah"

(Revelation 5:5). The reference to wine and grapes was a symbol of the great wealth Judah would have. And from a literal standpoint, the Judean Hills have many great wineries today.

Read Genesis 49:8–12.

After Jacob's death, Joseph and his brothers continued to live in Egypt. Joseph died at age 110. Prior to his death, he told his brothers that God would help them and lead them out of Egypt. In the book of Exodus, we are told that the descendants of the Israelites "became extremely powerful and filled the land" (Exodus 1:7 NLT).

When a new pharaoh came to power who knew nothing of Joseph and what he had done for Egypt, he became fearful of the Israelites. He was concerned that if Egypt was attacked by an enemy, the Israelites might assist them and overthrow his kingdom. So he enslaved the people and oppressed them with brutal slave masters, hoping they would actually die out. However, the more the Israelites were oppressed, the more they multiplied and spread.

As we read in Exodus 1:12–14, "But the more they afflicted them, the more they multiplied and grew. And they were grieved because of the children of Israel. And the Egyptians made the children of Israel to serve with rigour: And they made their lives bitter with hard bondage, in morter, and in brick, and in all manner of service in the field: all their service, wherein they made them serve, was with rigour."

Rigour is the British spelling for *rigor*, which speaks to the strictness, harshness, and severity with which the Hebrews were treated.

1526 BC—The Birth of Moses

The descendants of Jacob's son Levi were his son Kohath, followed by his grandson Amram. Amram had two sons, Moses and Aaron. The pharaoh in power when Moses was born gave an order to throw all the Hebrew male babies into the Nile River in an another attempt to control their growing population. It was also an attempt by Satan to prevent the promised Messiah from coming. Moses's mother was able to hide him for a time after he was born, but she knew he eventually would be discovered. So she put him in a waterproof basket and placed him in the Nile. When

Pharaoh's daughter came down to bathe in the river, she saw the basket and took pity on the child. Moses's sister had been watching Moses float down the river in the basket, and she asked the princess if she would like her to find a Hebrew woman to nurse the baby. The princess agreed. Moses's actual mother nursed him until he was older, at which point she took him back to the princess, who adopted Moses as her own son. She named him Moses, which means "to lift out."

Moses was raised as an Egyptian and educated in the court of Pharaoh. A number of years later, after Moses had grown up, he went out to see his own people. He saw how badly the Israelites were treated. When he saw an Egyptian beating one of his fellow Hebrews, Moses killed the Egyptian and hid his body in the sand. Pharaoh eventually heard what had happened and tried to kill Moses, but Moses fled to the land of Midian, east of the Sinai Peninsula.

Things continued to go badly for the Israelites in Egypt, and they cried out to God for help.

> And it came to pass in process of time, that the king of Egypt died: and the children of Israel sighed by reason of the bondage, and they cried, and their cry came up unto God by reason of the bondage. And God heard their groaning, and God remembered his covenant with Abraham, with Isaac, and with Jacob. And God looked upon the children of Israel, and God had respect unto them. (Exodus 2:23–25)

While Moses was shepherding his father-in-law's sheep, he came to Sinai to the "mountain of God." There, God appeared to him in a burning bush. Moses was amazed that although the bush was engulfed in flames, it did not burn up. He went to look closer, and God spoke to him from the bush. God told Moses not to come any closer and to take off his shoes because he was standing on holy ground. God identified himself as the God of Abraham, Isaac, and Jacob, and He told Moses that He had heard the cries of His people and was well aware of their suffering. Now, He was going to deliver them from the hands of Pharaoh, lead them out of Egypt, and give them a fertile land where the Canaanites, Hittites, Amorites, Perizzites, Hivites, and Jebusites were living. Then God dropped the bomb! He told Moses that He was sending him to Pharaoh to deliver the news that God wanted Pharaoh to let His people go. Of course Moses objected, but God would have none of it. Read Exodus 3:2–17.

God went on to tell Moses that He knew Pharaoh would not immediately let His people go, so He intended to raise His hand against him by performing all kinds of miracles. Eventually, the king would relent and let them go. And not only that, the Egyptians would actually give the Israelites articles made of silver and gold, as well as fine clothing.

Moses, accompanied by Aaron, went to Pharaoh, and everything God had told him came to pass. After the ten plagues—the last one being the death of all the firstborn sons of the Egyptians and their animals—Pharaoh finally relented and agreed to let the people go. God initiated the Passover to protect the firstborn of the Israelites from the tenth plague. He told them to sacrifice a lamb or goat and paint the doorposts of their homes with the blood. God promised protection for their firstborn sons if they did this. He also commanded them to celebrate the Festival of Unleavened Bread yearly to remind them of how God brought them out of Egypt with His strong hand. When they left Egypt, the Israelites asked the Egyptians for clothing and articles of silver and gold.

Exodus 12:36 states, "The Lord caused the Egyptians to look favorably on the Israelites, and they gave the Israelites whatever they asked for. So they stripped the Egyptians of their wealth!" (NLT). It happened exactly as God had predicted.

1446 BC—The Exodus from Egypt

The people of Israel had lived in Egypt for 430 years. In fact, it was on the last day of the 430th year that all the Lord's forces left the land. On this night the Lord kept his promise to bring his people out of the land of Egypt. So this night belongs to him, and it must be commemorated every year by all the Israelites, from generation to generation. (Exodus 12:40–42 NLT)

The Israelites miraculously escaped across the Red Sea, as God parted the water and allowed them to walk across on dry ground. But then Pharaoh (who had changed his mind) pursued with his entire army, and they were drowned when the water came crashing down on them.

"And Israel saw that great work which the Lord did upon the Egyptians: and the people feared the Lord, and believed the Lord, and his servant Moses" (Exodus 14:31).

Moses led the people to Mount Sinai in the wilderness of Sinai. They arrived exactly two months after they left Egypt. Over the course of those sixty days, God repeatedly tested His people and showed them that they could trust Him completely for everything they needed.

1445 BC—God Gives the Ten Commandments

Moses climbed the mountain to meet with God. God told Moses to tell the people how He had delivered them from the Egyptians and had brought them to Mount Sinai to be with Him. He told Moses to explain to them that if they would obey God and keep His covenant, then they would be God's own "peculiar [special] treasure," and they would become "a kingdom of priests, and an holy nation."

Read Exodus 19:3–6.

I have often wondered what it must have been like for all those people. They had lived for generations in Egypt. To some extent, they had adopted the Egyptian ways and even worshipped the Egyptian gods. It is important to note that each one of the ten plagues was the living God of the universe specifically challenging one or more of the false Egyptian gods and showing His superiority. Finally, in the tenth plague, God's death angel killed even Pharaoh's son. Pharaoh was considered to be divine, a descendant of the sun god Amun Ra. Hence, his son was considered to be divine offspring. In this series of battles, God against the Egyptian gods, the one true God showed His overwhelming superiority and power, over and over.

What many Christians fail to recognize is that what transpired at Mount Sinai was actually a wedding ceremony—God was marrying Israel, His bride. Try to put yourself there at the foot of Mount Sinai as I relate what happened. God told Moses to prepare the people for His arrival on the mountain in three days. So the people bathed themselves and washed their clothes, just as a bride would do. Then, on day three, while they were in the camp, a dense cloud came down over the mountain, along with thunder and lightning, followed by a long and probably deafening blast of a ram's horn. Then Moses brought the people to the mountain to meet with God. God had descended onto the mountain in the form of fire. Smoke billowed from the mountaintop like a giant furnace, and the whole mountain shook violently. The blast from the ram's horn got even louder! God called Moses to come up on the mountain, so he went up.

Read Exodus 19:16–20.

When Moses went up the mountain, God gave him the Ten Commandments.

The elements of the typical Jewish wedding were all there. The cloud over the mountain represented the *chuppah* (wedding veil), and the Ten Commandments were the *ketubah*, or marriage contract. I believe the lightning, thunder, and violent shaking of the mountain was God, the groom, impressing His bride!

It appears that Moses went up and down the mountain several times to consult with God. Once, when he was up on the mountain for forty days and nights, the people got restless. After having spent over four hundred years in Egypt, the Egyptian ways had become a part of them, including the worship of the Egyptian gods. The Israelites prevailed upon Aaron to built them a golden calf they could worship, which he did. God had delivered His people from the bondage of Egypt by taking them out of Egypt, but He still needed to take Egypt out of them.

The apostle Paul said that when the children of Israel left Egypt and passed through the Red Sea, it was like a baptism (1 Corinthians 10:1–4). God separated them and set them apart as His special people. To this very day, Jews celebrate Pesach (Passover), also called the Feast of Freedom, by having a seder meal. *Seder* means arrangement or order; hence, a seder meal is an orchestrated ceremonial meal. During the meal, four cups of wine are drunk. The four cups of wine are highly symbolic and very significant, for each one speaks of a need that God's people had that God solved. I want to take a moment to consider each cup of wine. Each has significance for the

Jews, but each also looked forward and prefigured something Christ would do for His followers.

The first cup is the *cup of sanctification*. The children of Israel were trapped in brutal slavery and needed deliverance. God took them out of Egypt, freeing them from slavery and setting them apart. But taking the people out of Egypt to Sinai was only the first step in their overall freedom.

The second cup is the *cup of deliverance*. The people had been slaves for over four hundred years and lived with a slave nature. This is very similar to prisoners who have been incarcerated for many years who are then set free. Unfortunately, due to their prison nature, they often don't adapt well to being free. They don't know how to live free, making their own decisions and providing for themselves. Many commit crimes simply to be reincarcerated so they don't have to deal with these issues. God also needed to deliver His people from "slave thinking" so they could live free of their slave nature.

The third cup is the *cup of redemption*. The people had been polluted by Egyptian idolatry, so they needed to be cleansed and forgiven of this sin. The final cup is the *cup of restoration*. The people were concerned that the Egyptians might come and force them back into slavery. But God promised He would be bound to them forever as their protector and leader.

For Christians, the cup of sanctification indicates our need to be freed from the power of Satan and suffering. When we are united with Jesus Christ, the righteousness of God is not only imputed (assigned) to us but imparted to us so that we have the power through the Holy Spirit to live right. The cup of deliverance is necessary due to the sin nature that dominates our thought lives, but when we accept Christ, we are given the mind of Christ and freed from the power of sin. The cup of redemption deals with the fact that we are filthy and sin-stained, but the blood of Christ cleanses and purifies us of our sin. Finally, the cup of restoration is our assurance that Satan will not recapture us. Jesus said He will drink this cup with us in the coming kingdom.

When Moses finally came down from the mountain and saw what was going on, he was furious. God judged the people, and three thousand died. Moses then interceded for the people, asking for forgiveness, which God granted. God then told Moses to get going and head for the Promised Land.

> And the Lord said unto Moses, "Depart, and go up hence, thou and the people which thou hast brought up out of the land of Egypt, unto the land which I sware unto Abraham, to Isaac, and to Jacob, saying, Unto thy seed will I give it: And I will send an angel before thee; and I will drive out the Canaanite, the Amorite, and the Hittite, and the Perizzite, the Hivite, and the Jebusite: Unto a land flowing with milk and honey: for I will not go up in the midst of thee; for thou art a stiffnecked people: lest I consume thee in the way." (Exodus 33:1–3)

This comment by God that the people were "stiffnecked" (stubborn and rebellious) was prophetic and played out repeatedly in the history of the children of Israel as their relationship with God fluctuated back and forth. Once again, Moses had to intercede on behalf of the people: "If you don't personally go with us, don't make us leave this place … For your presence among us sets your people and me apart from all other people on earth" (Exodus 33:15–16 NLT). Moses knew how essential God's presence would be for their success. Fortunately, God agreed to Moses's request.

During this time and with several trips up and down the mountain, God gave Moses elaborate instructions on the construction of the tabernacle (so God could live among His people) with all the intricate observances, as well as the all important observance of the Sabbath. Once the tabernacle was completed, we read the following in the final chapter of Exodus:

> Then a cloud covered the tent of the congregation, and the glory of the Lord filled the tabernacle. And Moses was not able to enter into the tent of the congregation, because the cloud abode thereon, and the glory of the Lord filled the tabernacle. And when the cloud was taken up from over the tabernacle, the children of Israel went onward in all their journeys: But if the cloud were not taken up, then they journeyed not till the day that it was taken up. For the cloud of the Lord was upon the tabernacle by day, and fire was on it by night, in the sight of all the house of Israel, throughout all their journeys. (Exodus 40:34–38)

So now the children of Israel were traveling toward the Promised Land, and God was living among His people by His presence in the tabernacle. When the cloud over the tabernacle lifted and moved, then the people traveled; otherwise, they stayed put. Similarly, if you are a Christian, you have been given the Holy Spirit, who lives within you—the very presence of God, which makes you a "new creature." Like the Israelites, do you allow your moves, day in and day out, to be led by the Holy Spirit, the presence of God within you?

One of my wife's favorite scripture verses is Proverbs 16:9: "The mind of a man plans his way, but the Lord directs his steps." Do you submit every minute of your day to God to direct?

1450–1410 BC—The Levitical Laws

Moses wrote the Levitical laws, under the direction of God, as a handbook for the priests and Levites. It outlined their duties in the worship of God and provided the standards for holy living that God desired from His people. It also gave specific instructions for the seasons and festivals (Passover and the Festival of Unleavened Bread, Festival of the Harvest, Festival of Trumpets, the Day of Atonement, Festival of Shelters, the Sabbath year, and the Year of Jubilee). In Leviticus 26, God promised the following blessings to Israel if they were obedient and kept their part of the covenant:

1. God would send seasonal rains in the spring and fall so the land would yield crops, and the trees would produce fruit.
2. They would live in peace and security in the land because God would give them victory over their enemies.
3. Multiply their people.
4. God said, "And I will walk among you, and will be your God, and ye shall be my people" (Leviticus 26:12).

However, if they chose not to listen to God and did not obey His commands by rejecting His decrees, then God promised the following:

1. God would bring terrors upon them—wasting diseases and fevers.
2. They would plant crops, but their enemies would eat them.

3. They would suffer defeat at the hands of their enemies.
4. They would run in fear, even when no one was chasing them.

Then, if they still did not obey in spite of all this, God promised to punish them "seven times over" in order to "break your proud spirit" (Leviticus 26:18–19). This punishment would include the following:

1. No rain would come, and therefore no crops would grow, and no trees would yield fruit.
2. God would allow wild animals to attack and carry off their children and kill their livestock.
3. Their population would decline.
4. If they persisted in disobedience, then they would be handed over to their enemies.
5. Famine would be so severe they would even eat their own children to survive.
6. God would destroy all their pagan shrines and make their cities desolate.
7. And finally, "And I will scatter you among the heathen, and will draw out a sword after you: and your land shall be desolate, and your cities waste" (Leviticus 26:33).
8. Those who survived would be demoralized as captives in foreign lands.

God's ultimate purpose in all this was not that He enjoyed punishing His people; quite the opposite. He wanted to bless them. Through His punishment, however, God knew that at last "their stubborn hearts will be humbled" (Leviticus 26:41). Once they had paid for all of their sins, God promised to remember His covenant with Abraham, Isaac, and Jacob. In verses 44–45, we read,

> And yet for all that, when they be in the land of their enemies, I will not cast them away, neither will I abhor them, to destroy them utterly, and to break my covenant with them: for I am the Lord their God. But I will for their sakes remember the covenant of their ancestors, whom I

brought forth out of the land of Egypt in the sight of the
heathen, that I might be their God: I am the Lord.

God had made an everlasting covenant with Israel, and He intended to
keep it.

1450–1410 BC—The Book of Numbers

The book of Numbers was also written by Moses during the forty years
the children of Israel wandered in the desert. Perhaps the key verses are
found in chapter 14.

Because all those men which have seen my glory, and
my miracles, which I did in Egypt and in the wilderness,
and have tempted me now these ten times, and have not
hearkened to my voice; Surely they shall not see the land
which I sware unto their fathers, neither shall any of them
that provoked me see it. (Numbers 14:22–23)

Over the years, the people recurrently complained and tested God.
So God told Moses that none of the original generation who had left
Egypt would enter the Promised Land. God decided that it would be more
appropriate for the next generation to go into the land.

During the forty years while the people rested and traveled, God gave
more instructions to Moses, which are recorded in Numbers. It was a very
difficult time for Moses, since the people often complained about any
number of things. It's tough to be a leader. As has often been said, "It's lonely
at the top of the mountain!"

As they approached the Promised Land, God told Moses to send out
twelve men as spies to explore the land of Canaan and report back. The
men explored the land for forty days. When they returned, they reported
how incredibly fruitful the land was. Ten of the men, however, were afraid
when they saw the size of some of the Canaanites, the descendants of Anak,
who were giants. Only Caleb, of the tribe of Judah, and Joshua, of the
tribe of Ephraim, wanted to go in and take the land. The ten men spread a
frightening report among the people, who wailed all night. Then the people

confronted Moses and Aaron, saying, "If only we had died in Egypt, or even here in the wilderness! ... Why is the Lord taking us to this country only to have us die in battle? ... Let's choose a new leader and go back to Egypt!" (Number 14:1–4 NLT).

Caleb and Joshua tried to encourage the people, but the people only wanted to stone them. God was angry with the people, and once again Moses interceded on their behalf. As previously stated, God told Moses that all of the people twenty years old and older would die in the wilderness; the only exceptions were Caleb and Joshua, who were allowed to enter Canaan.

If you travel to Israel today, you will observe the Orthodox Jews wearing tassels on the hems of their clothing. This was an instruction God gave to the people:

> And the Lord spake unto Moses, saying, "Speak unto the children of Israel, and bid them that they make them fringes in the borders of their garments throughout their generations, and that they put upon the fringe of the borders a ribband of blue: And it shall be unto you for a fringe, that ye may look upon it, and remember all the commandments of the Lord, and do them; and that ye seek not after your own heart and your own eyes, after which ye use to go a whoring: That ye may remember, and do all my commandments, and be holy unto your God. I am the Lord your God, which brought you out of the land of Egypt, to be your God: I am the Lord your God." (Numbers 15:37–41)

God knew they needed something as a continual reminder so they would follow Him. Unfortunately, as history would subsequently show, the people didn't keep their eyes on their tassels. However, even today Jews are reminded of these tassels every time they look at their national flag, which was adopted on October 28, 1948. The flag shows a blue Star of David on a white background between two horizontal blue strips and recalls the Jewish prayer shawl (tallit).

God gave Moses some interesting instructions in Numbers 19:1–10 regarding what was called the water of purification. First, they had to find a red heifer that was perfect and that had never been used for work. Second, the heifer was to be sacrificed outside the camp. Third, the ashes were to be collected and used for the ritual purification of an Israelite who had come in contact with a dead person. The Mishnah describes the ceremony of the burning of the red heifer that took place on the Mount of Olives. After the priest sacrificed the heifer, he sprinkled some of its blood in the direction of the temple seven times. It was then burned together with crimson-dyed wool, hyssop, and cedar wood, as God had instructed. From the time God gave the instructions to Moses until the Romans destroyed the second temple in Jerusalem, apparently only nine red heifers were ever sacrificed.

You're probably wondering why I have described this ceremony in such detail and what its relevance is today. According to Jewish law, one cannot participate in temple service without being ritually purified by the ashes of the red heifer. As I will describe in detail later, there is great interest in Israel now to rebuild the third temple in order to reestablish the sacrificial system. The Temple Institute in Jerusalem has been searching for a red heifer that meets the strict requirements. Such red heifers are quite rare. Attempts are being made to actually breed one. Some theologians have focused on the fact that the red heifer had to be slaughtered "without the camp" (i.e., outside the gate or city walls of Jerusalem). They believe this may be a reference to Jesus's being crucified outside the city walls: "Wherefore Jesus also, that he might sanctify the people with his own blood, suffered without the gate" (Hebrews 13:12).

Let us return to the wanderings of the Israelites, this time in the wilderness of Zin at Kadesh. Again, the people complained, this time because there was no water to drink. Again, they expressed that they wished they had died in Egypt. They questioned God, "And wherefore have ye made us to come up out of Egypt, to bring us in unto this evil place? it is no place of seed, or of figs, or of vines, or of pomegranates; neither is there any water to drink" (Numbers 20:5). God told Moses to speak to a rock so that it would spout water, but Moses was angry with the people, and he struck the rock twice with his staff because of the people's incessant complaining. Water gushed out, but God was not happy with Moses for striking the rock. He told Moses, "But the Lord said to Moses and Aaron, 'Because you did not trust me enough to demonstrate my holiness to the people of Israel, you will not lead them into the land I am giving them!'" (Numbers 20:12 NLT).

Also in Numbers 20, we read that the Edomites (descendants of Esau) refused to give the Israelites passage through their land, and the people had to travel around Edom. Once again, the Israelites complained, this time about the long journey. In response to the people's lack of trust, God sent poisonous snakes among the people, who died when bitten. The people realized they had sinned, and Moses prayed on their behalf. God told Moses to make a replica of a poisonous snake and attach it to a pole. Moses made a bronze replica of a poisonous snake and attached it to a pole; anyone who had been bitten and who looked at the bronze snake was healed. Although the Israelites did not know it, this foreshadowed Jesus. Jesus subsequently explained that He would be lifted up on a cross, and all who believed in Him would be saved from the power of death, in the way that the Israelites believed in the healing power of the bronze snake. (See John 3:14–15.)

Moses asked God to provide a new leader for Israel to replace him when he died. God selected Joshua, son of Nun, who, along with Caleb, had been one of the faithful spies who had explored the land of Canaan. God subsequently gave Moses the boundaries for the Promised Land in Numbers 34:1–12.

1407–1406 BC—The Book of Deuteronomy

After forty years of wandering in the desert, on a journey that should have taken eleven days, the people were finally ready to enter the Promised Land. God had used the time to test and prepare their hearts so "that he might make thee know that man doth not live by bread only, but by every word that proceedeth out of the mouth of the Lord doth man live" (Deuteronomy 8:3b). In this book, Moses started out by reviewing how God had cared for the people in order to encourage them to further trust Him in the future. Next, he reviewed the Ten Commandments and other laws given to them at Mount Sinai, stressing the consequences of disobedience. Finally, Moses challenged the people to not only know all the laws but to obey them. A good summary of Deuteronomy is given in chapter 7. Moses made it clear to the people that God did not choose them because they were a large nation; actually, they were the smallest. He chose them because He loved them, and He was keeping the oath He had made to their ancestors. Moses pointed out this was the reason why God had delivered them out of Egypt.

As such, they needed to never forget that He alone was God, and He would always be faithful to His covenant with them. However, Moses pointed out that this was conditional upon their obedience to all the instructions God had given them.

Read Deuteronomy 7:7–11.

Moses told the people that they did not need to be afraid for God would cross over the Jordan River ahead of them (Deuteronomy 9:3).

In Deuteronomy 17:14-20, God predicted a time would come when the people would not be satisfied with their theocracy (led by God) and would want a monarchy (led by a king) like all the other nations around them. So God gave four specific instructions for the king:

1. He must not build up a large stable of horses or send people to Egypt to buy horses.
2. He must not take many wives because they would turn his heart away from the Lord.
3. He must not accumulate large amounts of wealth in silver and gold.
4. He was to copy the book of the law, and as he sat on his throne, he was to read it daily so he would be able to direct the people properly regarding God's statutes. Additionally, this would prevent pride so that he would not turn away from God.

Did you get that? The king was to sit on his throne, copy God's Word for himself, and then read it every day for the rest of his life. By doing this, he would learn how to obey God properly, and it would prevent pride. Unfortunately, if you fast-forward to when Solomon became king, he broke or ignored all four of these instructions, and the nation suffered the consequences.

In Deuteronomy 30:1–8, Moses prophesied that the children of Israel would go into exile due to disobedience, but he encouraged them, when they were scattered and living in foreign countries, to remember all the instructions God had given them. If they did, then God would have mercy on them and gather them back from all the nations where they had been scattered. Interestingly, Moses went on to say,

And the Lord thy God will bring thee into the land which thy fathers possessed, and thou shalt possess it; and he will do thee good, and multiply thee above thy fathers. And the Lord thy God will circumcise thine heart, and the heart of thy seed, to love the Lord thy God with all thine heart, and with all thy soul, that thou mayest live. And the Lord thy God will put all these curses upon thine enemies, and on them that hate thee, which persecuted thee. And thou shalt return and obey the voice of the Lord, and do all his commandments which I command thee this day. (Deuteronomy 30:5–8)

When I first read this, I wondered, "What does it mean to circumcise a heart?" Unfortunately, many churches overemphasize salvation. There is no doubt that salvation with the forgiveness of sin is essential to our walk with God, but it's just the beginning; it doesn't end there. The Bible makes it clear that salvation involves a total transformation of our hearts, to the degree we each are called a "new creation." Many Christians assume that life is to be one of sinning and then asking for and receiving forgiveness, over and over. I even have seen Christians who use this as an excuse to sin. Now, I am not saying that we reach perfection and don't sin. But the apostle Paul made it quite clear that each of our lives should be one of progressive transformation in which we become more and more like Jesus. In Paul's letter to the church at Rome, he stated, "For those God foreknew he also predestined to be conformed to the likeness of his Son" (Romans 8:29). God has a much greater interest in each of us than just getting saved and going to heaven. A "new creation" is not left in bondage to sin. Part of becoming new creatures, made possible through Christ's death on the cross, is getting rid of the old sinful flesh (sin nature) by cutting it away, which is the process of spiritual circumcision. This spiritual circumcision is necessary because the flesh, our sin nature, delights in opposing God and sinning.

Christ's resurrection brought His power within us (the Holy Spirit), making it possible for us to choose between doing right and doing wrong. We are no longer dominated by the desire to sin. The change God brings about in our hearts actually makes us want to obey and do right. Just as physical circumcision was a mark of the old covenant, so too spiritual circumcision is a mark of the new covenant.

The children of Israel did go into exile in the Assyrian and Babylonian captivities and then again in AD 70 due to the Roman forces. It has been fascinating to see the reestablishment of the children of Israel in the Promised Land once again, ever since the United Nations' decision in 1947. But I am getting ahead of myself.

Moses's closing comments to the people are recorded in Deuteronomy as follows:

> And Moses made an end of speaking all these words to all Israel: And he said unto them, "Set your hearts unto all the words which I testify among you this day, which ye shall command your children to observe to do, all the words of this law. For it is not a vain thing for you; because it is your life: and through this thing ye shall prolong your days in the land, whither ye go over Jordan to possess it." (Deuteronomy 32:45–47)

It is not uncommon for those on their deathbeds to give words of advice to their loved ones. Similarly, Moses instructed the people with regard to how important God's words would be to their success or failure. He told them that God's words were literally their "life." It is no coincidence that the apostle John referred to Jesus as "the Word" (John 1:1, 14), and Jesus referred to Himself as "the way, the truth and the life" (John 14:6).

Moses then died on Mount Nebo in Moab.

1406 BC—The Hebrews Enter the Promised Land

The book of Joshua describes the history of Israel's conquest of the Promised Land (Canaan). It starts out with God's charge to Israel's new leader, Joshua.

> There shall not any man be able to stand before thee all the days of thy life: as I was with Moses, so I will be with thee: I will not fail thee, nor forsake thee. Be strong and of a good courage: for unto this people shalt thou divide for

an inheritance the land, which I sware unto their fathers to give them. Only be thou strong and very courageous, that thou mayest observe to do according to all the law, which Moses my servant commanded thee: turn not from it to the right hand or to the left, that thou mayest prosper withersoever thou goest. (Joshua 1:5–9)

Right off the bat, God gave Joshua the key to success. He was to "observe to do according to all the law." The law referred to God's words. If Joshua would simply pay special attention to God's words and obey them, God would guarantee Joshua's success. Sounds a lot like some of the things Jesus said. When He lived as God incarnate on earth, Jesus emphasized that He always sought to "not live by bread only, but by every word that proceedeth out of the mouth of the Lord doth man live" (Deuteronomy 8:3b; see also Matthew 4:4). There is a great truth here. Every morning I ask the Holy Spirit to not only enlighten me regarding the truths contained in God's Word but also to show me how to live by every one of God's words.

After seven years of military conquest, Israel finally controlled the Promised Land. As God had instructed, Joshua divided the land among the tribes of Israel. As an old man, he called the people together and gave his final instructions. He told them to be very careful to obey absolutely everything Moses had written down in the book of the law. They were not to associate with the pagan people in the land so that they would not be tempted in the worship of foreign gods. Rather, they were to "cleave unto the Lord your God" (i.e., hang on tightly to God). If they did this, then God would fight for them against their enemies, but if they turned away from God, it would spell disaster.

Read Joshua 23:6–16.

Here was a man who had devoted his entire life to serving God and who remained deeply committed to Him. Joshua was faithful to God, and God was faithful to Joshua, blessing him in everything he did throughout his life. Because of its importance, let me reiterate what he said. Joshua instructed the people to pay attention to everything that Moses had written down and to be very careful to obey *all* of it. He specifically told the people to "cleave" to God and not intermarry with the remnant of the foreign nations (the

Canaanites) in the Promised Land. This was because they were pagans and worshiped foreign gods. Both Joshua and God knew that if the people associated with them, they would be led astray, and it would lead to their downfall. Unfortunately, in the years to come, it did just that—repeatedly.

The bottom line here is very simple: *Cleave to God above all else, and make Him first in your life.* If you do, He promises to be with you, and if you live by His Word, every one of His words will provide "life" to your life.

This concept was so important to Joshua that before he died, he made a covenant with the people who agreed to obey all the instructions in the book of God's instructions. Then he died at age 110.

1375 BC—The Judges Begin to Rule Israel

The book of Judges always has been painful for me to read because it is a recurring cycle of the people abandoning God, and then, when they were reaping the consequences of their sin, they cried out to God for help. The book spans 325 years and records six such periods. After Joshua died, the nation had no powerful leader to whom it could look for guidance. The people struggled with incomplete obedience. They refused to completely eliminate the enemy from their land as they had been instructed to do, which led to intermarriage and idolatry. Everyone was doing that "which was right in his own eyes" (Judges 17:6). Sounds a lot like today, doesn't it? Due to God's incredible love and mercy, He sent twelve judges to deliver Israel in response to each cry for help.

The three best-known judges were Deborah (1209 BC), Gideon (1162 BC) and Samson (1105 BC).

1105 BC—The Birth of Samuel

Samuel was Israel's last judge who also became a priest and prophet. The Philistines captured the ark of the covenant, but it caused them so much trouble that they finally returned it. The people of Israel lamented that God had abandoned them. Samuel came to them and explained.

And Samuel spake unto all the house of Israel, saying, "If ye do return unto the Lord with all your hearts, then put away the strange gods and Ashtaroth from among you, and prepare your hearts unto the Lord, and serve him only: and he will deliver you out of the hand of the Philistines." Then the children of Israel did put away Baalim and Ashtaroth, and served the Lord only. (1 Samuel 7:3–4)

Do you see the recurring message here? It's nothing new—"Get rid of your idols and false gods and serve the one true God only!" When the Israelites did this, they defeated the Philistines and regained all the territory they had lost. Remember what Joshua told the people. If they would serve God only, then when they went into battle, it would be like one of them could defeat one thousand of the enemy (i.e., if God was with them in battle, they could not lose).

1050 BC— Saul Becomes Israel's First King (the Book of 1 Samuel)

Just as God had predicted, the time came when Israel wanted a king. Samuel warned them that if they crowned a king, that king would draft them into military service; force them to plow fields, harvest crops, and make weapons and chariot equipment; take the best of their lands for himself, demand a tenth of their flocks and harvests; and basically enslave them. But they wouldn't listen. They said, "That we also may be like all the nations; and that our king may judge us, and go out before us, and fight our battles" (1 Samuel 8:20).

Samuel anointed Saul as king. Saul had some successes, but eventually, due to Saul's disobedience, Samuel anointed David to be the next king. As a youth, David killed Goliath, a Philistine champion from Gath who was over nine feet tall and who had taunted the Israelite army for forty days. I love what David said when he faced Goliath.

Then said David to the Philistine, "Thou comest to me with a sword, and with a spear, and with a shield: but I come to thee in the name of the Lord of hosts, the God of the armies of Israel, whom thou hast defied. This day will the Lord deliver thee into mine hand; and I will smite thee, and take thine head from thee; and I will give the carcasses of the host of the Philistines this day unto the fowls of the air, and to the wild beasts of the earth; that all the earth may know that there is a God in Israel. And all this assembly shall know that the Lord saveth not with sword and spear: for the battle is the Lord's, and he will give you into our hands." (1 Samuel 17:45–47)

What great faith! It sounds almost brash and arrogant, but David was boasting about the strength and greatness of his God.

David went on to become a great warrior, and Saul became jealous of him. Eventually, Saul determined to kill David, so David fled. Saul pursued David. At one point, David was hiding in the back of a cave, and Saul came into the front of it to spend the night. While Saul was asleep, David cut off the tip of Saul's robe. The next day David showed the piece of robe to Saul and told him that he could have killed him but hadn't. Saul finally realized that David was destined to become king in his place. David promised not to harm Saul's family when he became king. Although David knew he would become king, he did not want to run ahead of God's timing. Unfortunately, Saul continued to pursue David. David even spared his life a second time. Eventually, the Philistines attacked Israel and defeated them. Saul was wounded severely by an arrow and fell on his sword to avoid being caught.

1010 BC—David Becomes Israel's King (the Book of 2 Samuel)

David reigned from 1010 to 970 BC. Second Samuel records the history of his reign. David was an incredible leader. He foreshadowed Christ, who would come as the perfect leader of a perfect kingdom. At the age of thirty, David was anointed king in Hebron. David led his men to Jerusalem and fought the Jebusites. He captured the fortress of Zion, which became known as the city of David and was where David made his home. David moved the ark of the covenant to Jerusalem.

The prophet Nathan came to David and declared that God was going to give him rest from his enemies, but he went on to make a messianic prophecy.

> For when you die and are buried with your ancestors, I will raise up one of your descendants, your own offspring, and I will make his kingdom strong. He is the one who will build a house—a temple—for my name. And I will secure his royal throne forever. I will be his father, and he will be my son. If he sins, I will correct and discipline him with the rod, like any father would do. But my favor will not be taken from him as I took it from Saul, whom I removed from your sight. Your house and your kingdom will continue before me for all time, and your throne will be secure forever. (2 Samuel 7:12–16 NLT)

When the apostle Peter preached to the crowd on the Day of Pentecost, he quoted some of these words (Acts 2:22–36; see also Psalm 16:8–11).

David went on to have a series of military victories that restored peace to Israel. However, he committed adultery with Bathsheba and had her husband, Uriah, killed in battle. Nathan confronted David and told him that as a result of his sin, "Now therefore the sword shall never depart from thine house; because thou hast despised me, and hast taken the wife of Uriah the Hittite to be thy wife. Thus saith the Lord, Behold, I will raise up evil against thee out of thine own house, and I will take thy wives before thine eyes, and give them unto thy neighbour, and he shall lie with thy wives in the sight of this sun" (2 Samuel 12:10–11). Bathsheba gave birth to a child, but the child died. She became pregnant again, however, and gave birth to a son whom they named Solomon.

Nathan's prophecies came to pass when Tamar, the sister of Absalom, one of David's sons, was raped by her half brother Ammon. Absalom avenged the rape by killing Ammon. Later, Absalom led a rebellion against David. He even went so far as to sleep with David's concubines in a tent on the palace roof in plain sight of everyone, just as Nathan had prophesied. He raised an army against David, but Joab defeated him, and Absalom was killed.

970 BC—Solomon Becomes Israel's King

As an old man, David made his son Solomon king and gave him these final instructions:

> Now the days of David drew nigh that he should die; and he charged Solomon his son, saying, "I go the way of all the earth: be thou strong therefore, and shew thyself a man; And keep the charge of the Lord thy God, to walk in his ways, to keep his statutes, and his commandments, and his judgments, and his testimonies, as it is written in the law of Moses, that thou mayest prosper in all that thou doest, and whithersoever thou turnest thyself: That the Lord may continue his word which he spake concerning me, saying, 'If thy children take heed to their way, to walk before me in truth with all their heart and with all their soul, there shall not fail thee (said he) a man on the throne of Israel.'" (1 Kings 2:1–4)

These instructions sound a lot like Joshua's final words. David had come to realize exactly what Joshua had; that is, in order to prosper in life you need to "keep the charge of the Lord thy God"—know His laws and walk in them.

Shortly after Solomon became king, God appeared to him in a dream and asked him, "What do you want?"

Solomon replied, "And now, O Lord my God, thou hast made thy servant king instead of David my father: and I am but a little child: I know not how to go out or come in. And thy servant is in the midst of thy people which thou hast chosen, a great people, that cannot be numbered nor counted for multitude. Give therefore thy servant an understanding heart to judge thy people, that I may discern between good and bad: for who is able to judge this thy so great a people?" (1 Kings 3:7–9). God was pleased Solomon had asked for wisdom so he could be a good leader. As a result, God promised him not only wisdom but also that for which he did not ask—riches and fame. God also added, "And if thou wilt walk in my ways, to keep my statutes and my commandments, as thy father David did walk, then I will lengthen thy days" (1 Kings 3:14).

There it is again—obedience is the key to life, even a long life. Solomon went on to build the temple in Jerusalem (completed in 959 BC), as well as a grand palace. When the ark of the covenant was brought into the temple, God's presence filled the Holy of Holies, and Solomon prayed a wonderful prayer of dedication. God appeared to Solomon a second time and told him,

> And if thou wilt walk before me, as David thy father walked, in integrity of heart, and in uprightness, to do according to all that I have commanded thee, and wilt keep my statutes and my judgments: Then I will establish the throne of thy kingdom upon Israel for ever, as I promised to David thy father, saying, There shall not fail thee a man upon the throne of Israel. But if ye shall at all turn from following me, ye or your children, and will not keep my commandments and my statutes which I have set before you, but go and serve other gods, and worship them: Then will I cut off Israel out of the land which I have given them; and this house, which I have hallowed for my name, will I cast out of my sight; and Israel shall be a proverb and a byword among all people: And at this house, which is high, every one that passeth by it shall be astonished, and shall hiss; and they shall say, "Why hath the Lord done thus unto this land, and to this house?" And they shall answer, "Because they forsook the Lord their God, who brought forth their fathers out of the land of Egypt, and have taken hold upon other gods, and have worshipped them, and served them: therefore hath the Lord brought upon them all this evil."
> (1 Kings 9:4–9)

This was, in essence, a prophetic message, as the temple subsequently would be destroyed twice—first by the Babylonians and second by the Romans.

Solomon became Israel's grandest king, but he failed miserably with regard to the instructions God had given to Moses in Deuteronomy 17. He amassed incredible wealth and built a huge force of chariots and horses (many imported from Egypt). He loved foreign women, whom he married—he had seven hundred wives and three hundred concubines. We have no record that he copied God's instructions and referred to them daily. As expected, the foreign women begged him to engage in the worship of their foreign gods. He resisted initially, then tolerated it, and finally participated in worship. He even built pagan shrines on the Mount of Olives to the detestable gods Chemosh (god of Moab) and Molech (god of the Ammonites). Since Solomon abandoned God, worshiped foreign gods, and did not obey God's decrees and regulations like his father, David, had done, God said, "Behold, I will rend the kingdom out of the hand of Solomon" (1 Kings 11:31).

Solomon ruled for forty years. When he died, his son Rehoboam became king.

930 BC—The Kingdom of Israel Is Divided into the Northern Kingdom of Israel and the Southern Kingdom of Judah

We now enter a very dark period for the nation of Israel. The northern ten tribes (northern kingdom) of Israel, led by Jeroboam, one of Solomon's prior officials, revolted. He set up his capital in Shechem in the hill country of Ephraim. Rehoboam ruled Judah (the southern kingdom), which included the tribes of Judah and Benjamin. The northern and southern kingdoms were both ruled by a series of kings, most of whom were evil and who led the people away from God and into pagan practices. A few kings, however, instituted reforms and led the Israelites back to God, but in the end, it was not enough.

This was a very important time for the children of Israel. During this period of more than three hundred years, the major prophets—Isaiah, Jeremiah, Ezekiel, and Daniel—prophesied, as did the minor prophets (Hosea, Joel, Amos, Obadiah, Jonah, Micah, Nahum, Habakkuk, Zephaniah, Haggai, Zechariah, and Malachi). These prophets spoke into the lives of the kings and people as God's way of trying to draw the people back and spare them from the judgment to come.

Despite all this, however, both kingdoms fell, and the people were taken into captivity. The northern kingdom was overcome by the Assyrians and led into captivity in 721 BC. Similarly, the southern kingdom was conquered by the Babylonians and led into captivity in 585 BC. The ten tribes of the northern kingdom never returned to the Promised Land, but the southern kingdom, after spending seventy years in Babylonian captivity, was then permitted to return.

The Medo-Persian army conquered the Babylonians in 539 BC. When Cyrus became king of Persia, he allowed the Jews to return to Israel. Zerubbabel led the first return in 538 BC, Ezra led the second in 458 BC, and Nehemiah led the third in 445 BC. The temple was rebuilt (called the second temple), although it was not even close to its former grandeur, and the walls of the city of Jerusalem were restored, providing protection for the people living in Jerusalem.

Esther was an orphan who lived among the Jewish exiles in Persia under the protection of her cousin Mordecai. King Xerxes the Great (in Hebrew, *Ahasuerus*), the fifth king of Persia, ruled from 486 to 465 BC, and Esther became his queen in 479 BC. At one point, Haman, a vizier (high-ranking political advisor) in Persia, demanded that Mordecai bow down and prostrate himself before him. Mordecai refused, which infuriated Haman. Haman found out that Mordecai was a Jew, so he devised a plot to destroy all the Jews living in Persia. Haman convinced the king to go along with his extermination plan by explaining that the Jews refused to obey their law. He also offered to deposit 375 tons of silver in the royal treasury!

The king signed a decree that all Jews would be slaughtered in a single day. They cast lots (called *purim*) to determine on which day this would occur. When Mordecai heard about the decree, he convinced Esther that she needed to go before the king. For even the queen to go before the king without being summoned could mean death. Esther fasted for three days and then went to the king. Fortunately, she was well received. She had devised her own plan and invited both the king and Haman to a banquet. The dinner went well, and Esther asked them to return the next night.

In the meantime, the king remembered that Mordecai had saved his life by exposing an assassination plot, so he honored him the next day. That night at the second banquet, the king asked Esther what she requested. She exposed Haman's evil plot, and the king had him executed. Subsequently, on the day the Jews were to be slaughtered, they defended themselves and overpowered their enemies. Ever since then, the Jews have celebrated the festival of Purim, which commemorates the salvation of the Jewish people while living in Persia.

This was not the first time or the last that Satan would use human envoys to try to annihilate the Jewish people. Ancient Egypt, the Philistines, the Assyrian Empire, the Babylonian Empire, the Persian Empire, the Greek Empire, the Roman Empire, the Byzantine Empire, the Crusaders, the Spanish Empire, Nazi Germany, and the Soviet Union all have waged war on the Jews, some with attempts at annihilation. Where are they today? Gone.

Despite the exile, the people of Judah had not learned their lesson and still did not listen to the prophets in the postexile period. The priests did not obey and honor God's directives for proper worship and sacrifices. Men divorced their wives and married younger pagan women, which was frank disobedience to God's law and very destructive to their children's religious training. Malachi was the last of the Old Testament prophets. He told the priests, "But ye are departed out of the way; ye have caused many to stumble at the law; ye have corrupted the covenant of Levi, saith the Lord of hosts" (Malachi 2:8). Through Malachi, God called the people to repentance. "'Ever since the days of your ancestors, you have scorned my decrees and failed to obey them. Now return to me, and I will return to you,' says the Lord of Heaven's Armies. 'But you ask, "How can we return when we have never gone away?"'" (Malachi 3:7 NLT). What incredible spiritual blindness!

He confronted the people who had neglected the temple and participated in profane worship. Things got so bad that God spoke to Malachi, saying,

> "How I wish one of you would shut the Temple doors so that these worthless sacrifices could not be offered! I am not pleased with you," says the Lord of Heaven's Armies, "and I will not accept your offerings. But my name is honored by people of other nations from morning till night. All around the world they offer sweet incense and pure offerings in honor of my name. For my name is great among the nations," says the Lord of Heaven's Armies. (Malachi 1:10–11 NLT)

Yet there was a small remnant of people who continued to be faithful to God.

> Then they that feared the Lord spake often one to another: and the Lord hearkened, and heard it, and a book of remembrance was written before him for them that feared the Lord, and that thought upon his name. "And they shall be mine, saith the Lord of hosts, in that day when I make up my jewels; and I will spare them, as a man spareth his own son that serveth him. Then shall ye return, and discern between the righteous and the wicked, between him that serveth God and him that serveth him not." (Malachi 3:16–18)

Despite the impending judgment due to their sin, as always, God promised hope. He promised to send two messengers (Malachi 3:1–5). The first messenger would prepare the way for the second. The first is considered to be John the Baptist, who subsequently came to prepare the way for the second messenger, Jesus the Messiah. After Malachi, the nation of Israel heard nothing from God for over four hundred years. Then the two messengers came!

The Covenants

Before we move on to the messianic prophecies, I want to take a moment to summarize and reflect on the covenants that God made with the Israelites. In the series of covenants, we see not only God's plan of redemption for all of mankind but His deep desire to be in a relationship with man, the pinnacle of His creation.

Abrahamic covenant: In this covenant God promised three things:

1. Land—First, God said it was the land God would show Abram (Genesis 12:1); second, it was the land Abram could actually see by looking around (Genesis 13:14–18); and finally, God gave the exact dimensions of the land (Genesis 15:18–21), stating the boundaries would be between the Nile River and the Euphrates River. Then, in

Genesis 17:8 it states, "And I will give unto thee, and to thy seed after thee, the land wherein thou art a stranger, all the land of Canaan, for an everlasting possession; and I will be their God." I want to point out that the land of Canaan is immeasurably smaller than what was promised in Genesis 15. Only under King David did the Israelites come close to conquering what was promised in Genesis 17. So what are we to make of this? It soon will become clear.

2. Descendants—God told Abram his descendants would become a great nation (Genesis 12:2; 17:6). Later, God further specified to King David, "And thine house and thy kingdom shall be established for ever before thee: thy throne shall be established for ever" (2 Samuel 7:16). Within this promise was a look forward to the future messianic kingdom. The rule of Jesus the Messiah and coming King will be everlasting.

3. Blessing—"And I will make of thee a great nation, and I will bless thee, and make thy name great; and thou shalt be a blessing: And I will bless them that bless thee, and curse him that curseth thee: and in thee shall all families of the earth be blessed" (Genesis 12:2–3). Notice that God promised to bless Abram, and through his descendants, the whole world would be blessed. This was to manifest in two ways: (1) the Messiah to come, who would be a descendant of Abram, would be a blessing to all mankind; and (2) the Israelites themselves were to be a blessing to the people around them. Unfortunately, they were often self-absorbed (much like we are today) and forgot this. It is essential for us to note that this principle of being a blessing to others extends to all Christians, who the Bible says have been grafted into the root of Israel (Romans 11:17–18).

Let's return to my question regarding the extent of the land God promised to Abram. Since Israel never completely occupied or controlled even the boundary specified for the land of Canaan, let alone from the Nile to the Euphrates, does that mean God lied? Of course not! I have found that when reading prophecy, it often must be understood in a sequential sense. This means that a prophecy often has a present-tense meaning, sometimes a messianic prediction, and a future end-time meaning, all rolled into one.

Abram was shown the land his descendants would one day possess. Under King David, the Israelites almost—but never fully—occupied the land of Canaan. They never fully controlled it, even though they ruled over it. Hence, what God promised remains to be fulfilled in the future. As we explore the many prophecies regarding Israel in the sections ahead, we will see how God's promises will be fulfilled.

Mosaic (Sinai) covenant: This is also referred to as the Old Covenant.

1. Law—Obedience to the law was required in order for the Israelites to receive the blessings God promised. God gave them a choice: If they obeyed, life would be good, but if they disobeyed, life would be bad, and they would receive cursings instead of blessings. By their obedience, God wanted the children of Israel, His chosen people, to be a light to the dark world around them.
2. The sacrificial system—This system looked forward to the perfect sacrifice Jesus Christ, our Pascal Lamb, who would bear the sin of the world and through whom all could be saved.

The purpose of the law was to show the Israelites their sinfulness so that they would recognize their need for the Messiah, their Savior. Their pride led them to believe that by actually performing all the rituals the law required, they could somehow save themselves. They missed the principle that would become clearer with the new covenant—that salvation comes by faith in God, not by keeping the law.

Today, as Christians under the new covenant, we are to be lights in the dark world in which we live. Jesus came as the light of the world, and when we are saved and the Holy Spirit enters us, making each of us a new creation, we are to shine in the midst of darkness. We are to look and act differently in comparison to those living in the world around us. The world should see something different in us, which is attractive. Those around us should wonder, "Why don't I have the peace and the joy that person has?" Hopefully, that will lead to conversations in which we are asked why we are so different. As Saint Francis of Assisi said, "Preach the Gospel at all times, and if necessary use words."

Davidic covenant: In 2 Samuel 7, God promised the following:

1. The Messiah would come through David's descendants. Subsequently, when Jesus came and entered Jerusalem on Palm Sunday, the crowds cried out, "Hosanna to the son of David: Blessed is he that cometh in the name of the Lord; Hosanna in the highest" (Matthew 21:9). This was a fulfillment of what Samuel had prophesied.
2. There would be an everlasting messianic kingdom (1 Chronicles 17:11–14).
3. The promise of land was reaffirmed.

The new covenant: The new covenant with the coming of the Messiah was predicted many times throughout the Old Testament. God promised Israel a number of things. A partial summary was given by Ezekiel:

> For I will take you from among the heathen, and gather you out of all countries, and will bring you into your own land. Then will I sprinkle clean water upon you, and ye shall be clean: from all your filthiness, and from all your idols, will I cleanse you. A new heart also will I give you, and a new spirit will I put within you: and I will take away the stony heart out of your flesh, and I will give you an heart of flesh. And I will put my spirit within you, and cause you to walk in my statutes, and ye shall keep my judgments, and do them. And ye shall dwell in the land that I gave to your fathers; and ye shall be my people, and I will be your God. (Ezekiel 36:24–28)

So what God promised was this:

1. A regathering of the children of Israel from all the countries where they are scattered, back to the land of Israel, where they will live forever.
2. A cleansing from the filthiness of their idolatrous worship.

3. A spiritual transformation in which they are given new hearts. I like to think of this as a heart transplant. God realized that man needed an inner transformation. Jeremiah phrased it this way: "I will put my instructions deep within them, and I will write them on their hearts" (Jeremiah 31:33 NLT).

4. The placement of God's Holy Spirit within them so they could finally obey His statutes. Ezekiel 37:21–28 gives these additional promises:

5. The kingdoms of Judah and Israel will no longer be divided but will be one nation ruled by one King—Jesus—forever.

6. God will dwell in their midst forever.

7. God will make an everlasting covenant of peace with them.

What God promised in the new covenant was a relationship with man quite different from what it had been. The relationship under the old covenant was more corporate in nature, but the relationship promised by the new covenant was to be personal. Under the old sacrificial system, the blood of animals could never completely atone for sin, but through Jesus's death and resurrection, His blood could fully and completely atone for human sin and hence restore man's broken fellowship with God (Hebrews 9:13–15).

In Acts 2, on the Day of Pentecost, the Holy Spirit fell on the Jewish believers who were gathered together. Peter preached that day and explained that Jesus was the promised Messiah and that the Old Testament prophecies had been fulfilled in Him. He went on to say that this filling of the Holy Spirit was a fulfillment of what the prophet Joel had prophesied. "And it shall come to pass afterward, that I will pour out my spirit upon all flesh ... And also upon the servants and upon the handmaids in those days will I pour out my spirit" (Joel 2:28–29).

Additionally, in Acts 10, God instructed Peter to go to Caesarea to the house of Cornelius, a Roman army officer. They received the message Peter preached about who Jesus was, and when they received Jesus, the Holy Spirit also fell upon them. Through this, God showed Peter that under the new covenant, salvation was available also to the Gentiles.

I love what Peter stated: "Then Peter replied, 'I see very clearly that God shows no favoritism. In every nation he accepts those who fear him and do what is right. This is the message of Good News for the people of

Israel—that there is peace with God through Jesus Christ, who is Lord of all'" (Acts 10:34–36 NLT).

The writer of Hebrews contrasted the old and new covenants in chapter 8. He explained how much better the new covenant was and that the law of the old covenant was written on stone tablets, but the new covenant of grace was written on the hearts and in the minds of men and women.

The apostle Paul clarified and explained on many occasions the nature of this new covenant. He emphasized that we are saved by faith and not by works and that salvation is the free gift of God. He spoke of how the Holy Spirit lives within us, giving us life (Romans 8:10–11).

The new covenant was ushered in by Jesus's death and resurrection and became manifest with the outpouring of His Spirit on the Day of Pentecost. Ever since then, countless millions have accepted Christ as Savior and made Him Lord of their lives. In that sense, many of the Old Testament prophecies have been fulfilled, but the seven aspects of the new covenant regarding Israel, although having an initial partial fulfillment on the Day of Pentecost, also have an end-time fulfillment. Since 1947 we have seen the return and regathering of the Israelites to the land of Israel. There is also a growing messianic movement, with many Jews accepting Jesus, Yeshua, as the Messiah.

But this is just the beginning.

PART 4
Old Testament
Messianic Prophecies

The Old Testament books were written between 1450 BC and 430 BC, and they contain over four hundred messianic prophecies—prophecies concerning Jesus Christ, the Messiah. Psalm 22 was written by David around one thousand years before Christ and contains eleven specific predictions about the Crucifixion of Jesus, which occurred exactly as predicted! Similarly, Isaiah, writing some seven hundred years before Christ, made striking predictions about Jesus's persecution and death that were also fulfilled.

Before we consider the messianic prophecies, let's be clear on who the Bible says Jesus Christ, the Messiah, was and is. Yeshua (Jesus, in Hebrew) was born in Bethlehem, Israel, to Jewish parents. His first followers were all Jews. The first messianic prophecy was right after the fall of man, when God told Satan a time would come when he would be crushed by the "seed" of a woman (Genesis 3:15). The prophecies clearly state that Jesus would be born of a virgin, which occurred when the Holy Spirit came upon Mary and fertilized her seed (egg). This was called the incarnation. Hence, Jesus was born both the Son of Man and the Son of God. When God made a covenant with Abram in Genesis 12:1–3, He told Abram, "and in thee shall all the families of the earth be blessed." Jesus subsequently came as the Savior of the entire world, fulfilling this promise. Jesus's ministry on earth was to His own people, the Jews (Matthew 15:24), but the salvation He brought through His death and resurrection was for all people.

I have listed a number of what I believe are the most significant prophecies about the Messiah in the following table. Remember, these were written four hundred to one thousand years before they came to pass! The authenticity of Isaiah's prophecies, in particular, were given significant confirmation in 1947, when the Dead Sea Scrolls were discovered in caves in Qumran by a Bedouin shepherd. The Great Scroll of Isaiah contains the entire book of Isaiah and has been determined by scientists to have been written in 100 BC or even earlier. The scroll was written in Hebrew and is virtually identical to our modern texts.

Prophecies Concerning the Messiah	Old Testament Prophecy	New Testament Fulfillment
Jesus would be born of a virgin.	Isaiah 7:14	Matthew 1:18–25 Luke 1:26–35
The Messiah would be the offspring of the woman.	Genesis 3:15	Galatians 4:4
The Messiah would be a descendant of Abraham.	Genesis 12:3	Acts 3:24–26
The Messiah would be a descendant of David.	2 Samuel 7:12–16	Matthew 1:1 Luke 1:32–33
The Messiah would be born in Bethlehem.	Micah 5:2	Matthew 2:1–6
The Messiah would be preceded by a forerunner (John the Baptist).	Isaiah 40:3–5	Matthew 3:1–3 Mark 1:1–2 John 1:22–23

Prophecies Concerning the Messiah	Old Testament Prophecy	New Testament Fulfillment
Jesus would be a great light.	Isaiah 9:1–2	Matthew 4:13–16
Jesus would be the light of the world.	Malachi 3:1 Isaiah 42:1–6	Matthew 11:10 John 8:12
Jesus would be called the Son of God.	Psalm 2:1–12	Mark 1:11 Luke 3:22 Hebrews 1:5; 5:5
Jesus would be called the Son of Man	Daniel 7:13–14	Matthew 9:6; 12:8; 13:41 Mark 8:31 Luke 9:22
Daniel predicted the time of Jesus's first coming and Crucifixion.	Daniel 9:24-27	Galatians 4:4
The Messiah would be the wonderful Counselor, mighty God, everlasting Father, and Prince of Peace.	Isaiah 9:6–7	Luke 1:32–33 Acts 10:36 Romans 9:5
Jesus would be a prophet, like Moses.	Deuteronomy 18:15–19	Matthew 21:46 Luke 24:19 John 6:14; 7:40 Acts 3:22

Prophecies Concerning the Messiah	Old Testament Prophecy	New Testament Fulfillment
The Messiah would perform healing.	Isaiah 35:5–6	Matthew 11:4–6
The Messiah would proclaim good news to the poor.	Isaiah 61:1–2	Luke 4:17–21
The Messiah would come riding into Jerusalem on a colt.	Zechariah 9:9	Matthew 21:1–7
Jesus would enter the temple with authority.	Malachi 3:1	Matthew 21:12 Luke 19:45
The Messiah would come as the suffering servant.	Isaiah 52:13–53:12	Matthew 8:16–17; 20:28 Mark 10:45
Jesus would be betrayed for thirty pieces of silver.	Zechariah 11:12–13	Matthew 26:14–15; 27:3, 9–10
The Messiah would be killed.	Isaiah 53:5–9	Matthew 27:50 Mark 15:37–39
The Messiah would be lifted up.	Numbers 21:6–9	John 3:14–18
The Crucifixion experience	Psalm 22	Matthew 27:34–50 John 19:17–30
The Messiah would be pierced.	Zechariah 12:10	John 19:31–37 Revelation 1:7

Prophecies Concerning the Messiah	Old Testament Prophecy	New Testament Fulfillment
The Messiah's legs would not be broken.	Psalm 22:17 Psalm 34:20	John 19:31–36
Jesus would be the Passover Lamb.	Exodus 12:1–51	John 1:29, 36 1 Corinthians 5:7–8 1 Peter 1:19
Jesus would be forsaken by His disciples.	Zechariah 13:7	Matthew 26:31, 56
The Messiah would be buried with the rich.	Isaiah 53:9	Matthew 27:59–60 Mark 15:46
Jesus would be resurrected.	Psalm 16:8–11	Acts 2:22–32; 13:35–37
Jesus would bring in the new covenant.	Jeremiah 31:31	Luke 22:20 1 Corinthians 11:25 Hebrews 12:24
Jesus would ascend into heaven and sit at God's right hand.	Psalm 68:18	Luke 24:51 Acts 1:9

I would suggest you spend some time looking up the Old Testament prophecies and then reading their New Testament fulfillments. A good devotional exercise would be to take one daily for a month, until you work your way through them.

The fact that Jesus has fulfilled so many of the Old Testament prophecies should give us the confidence to believe the many other prophecies that remain to be fulfilled. Here are just a few:

Old and New Testament Prophecies to Be Fulfilled	Scripture
He will bring peace to the world.	Isaiah 2:1–4
The entire world will acknowledge God as the one true God.	Zechariah 14:9
The leopard will lie down with the goat and calf.	Isaiah 11:6–7
The lion will eat straw like the ox.	Isaiah 65:25
Jesus will destroy Israel's enemies.	Isaiah 29:4–6; 42:13
There will be no more war.	Micah 4:2–3
Jesus will rule the nations from Jerusalem.	Micah 4:3
Jesus will return as the Lion of Judah to judge the world.	Revelation 19:11–15

PART 5
Old Testament Prophecy Regarding Past, Present, and Future Events

We have considered a number of prophecies and have seen God's faithfulness in seeing them fulfilled. Now I want to look at the prophecies in detail. I believe you will be amazed by what you will read.

We will begin by looking at the prophecies made by the prophet Daniel. Daniel was exiled to Babylon, and while he was there, he received three visions regarding empires that would rule the world. His three visions are chronicled in Daniel 2, 7, and 8. I will summarize what Daniel predicted and what subsequently occurred.

Daniel was likely in his sixties when he received the first vision, sometime around 553 BC. Each of the three visions used a different metaphor to describe the same thing. In Daniel 2, Nebuchadnezzar, the Babylonian king, had a dream of a large statue, which represented four kingdoms that would rule the world. He did not know what the dream meant. Daniel prayed, and God revealed the dream and its meaning to him in a vision.

During the reign of the next Babylonian king, Belshazzar, Daniel had a dream in which he saw a great storm that was churning up the sea, and then four beasts came out of the sea, each representing a different world empire.

Finally, in the third year of King Belshazzar's reign, Daniel saw another vision, this time of three animals. You can see the similarity of the visions in the following chart. I have compared the three metaphors and the different kingdoms they symbolized.

Daniel	Chapter 2 Large shining statue of a man with:	Chapter 7	Chapter 8
Babylonian Empire (606–539 BC)	Gold head	Lion with eagle's wings.	Lion with eagle's wings
Medo-Persian Empire (539–331 BC)	Chest and arms of silver	Bear	Ram with two horns
Greek Empire (331–146 BC)	Bronze belly and thighs	Leopard with four wings and four heads	Male goat with large horn broken into four horns
Roman Empire (146 BC–AD 476)	Iron legs and iron/clay feet	Beast with huge iron teeth, bronze claws, and ten horns	Small horn

Let me summarize these four kingdoms and some of the relevant prophecies concerning each one.

Babylonian Empire: Nebuchadnezzar ruled as a king, and his kingdom was an absolute monarchy with centralization of power.

The prophet Jeremiah (625–586 BC) prophesied that Babylon would rule Judah for seventy years, which began in 597 BC. He also prophesied that Babylon subsequently would be conquered and become a "wasteland forever" (Jeremiah 25:11–12 NLT) and that it would be "desolate forever. Even your stones will never again be used for building" (Jeremiah 51:24–26 NLT). Similarly, Isaiah had previously prophesied (701–681 BC) the following:

1. The Medes would attack Babylon, and it would never be inhabited again (Isaiah 13:17–22).
2. Cyrus would divert the Euphrates River and take Babylon (Isaiah 45:1).
3. Babylon would be reduced to a swampland (Isaiah 14:23).

Incredibly, every one of these prophecies was fulfilled, and ever since, the name Babylon has been used as a metaphor for all who oppose God. Revelation and many other Old Testament prophecies speak of Babylon (meaning all evil and all who oppose God) in the end times and that it will be removed from the earth.

Medo-Persian Empire: As I stated previously, in 539 BC, the Persian king Cyrus conquered Babylon, and in 538 BC, he gave permission for the Jews in captivity to return to the Promised Land. The Medo-Persian Empire was a monarchial oligarchy with nobles.

The prophet Ezekiel prophesied to the Jews in exile in Babylonia after the defeat of King Jehoiachin. He was exiled there in 597 BC. In Ezekiel 36 and 47, Ezekiel prophesied that Israel, as a whole (both northern and southern kingdoms), would return to Palestine. He spoke of a more complete returning of the Jews to the Holy Land, as compared to what occurred after the Babylonian captivity, when only Judah (southern kingdom) returned. This return prefigured the complete return of the Jews that has occurred since 1948 and will continue to occur.

Greek Empire: Alexander the Great conquered the Medo-Persian Empire in 331 BC. As a result of his swift and extensive military campaigns, he became the world ruler. When he died, his empire was divided into four main parts.

Roman Empire: Rome was ruled by Caesar and the senate, which represented a form of democratic imperialism. Rome finally defeated the remains of the Greek Empire in 146 BC. As we will see, Daniel's metaphors of this empire represented not only the original Roman Empire but the future Neo-Roman Empire to come in the last days.

God revealed to two Babylonian kings and to Daniel the four successive kingdoms that would rule the world. Any one of the visions would have been remarkable, but to have three is incredible. Remember, if it's repeated in scripture, it's important. And equally as amazing, in Daniel 11, God revealed to Daniel, with remarkable detail, the future reign of Persian and Greek leaders.

Daniel's Seventy Weeks

Perhaps one of the most difficult prophesies in the Bible is recorded in Daniel 9. In verses 20–22, we find Daniel praying and pleading with God. He was confessing not only his sins but also the sins of the Jewish people. Suddenly, the angel Gabriel appeared to him in response to his prayers. Gabriel said, "I am now come forth to give you skill [insight] and understanding." Gabriel explained there would be seventy weeks of seven, which equaled 490. Each day in each of the weeks is thought to represent one year, or 490 years. The purpose of the vision was to reveal that the seventy weeks of seven (490 years) were decreed by God for the Jews to do the following:

1. Finish their rebellion.
2. Put an end to their sin.
3. Atone for their guilt (accomplished through the cross).
4. Bring in everlasting righteousness; that is, a new order of security brought in by the Messiah.
5. Confirm (seal up) the prophetic vision that would culminate in the reign of the Messiah.
6. Anoint the most high place (i.e., the temple).

The Second Coming of Christ occurs within these.

The first sixty-nine weeks began when the command was given to rebuild Jerusalem in 445 BC. In Daniel's time, Israel used a 360-day year. In 538 BC, Cyrus gave the first decree that permitted Zerubbabel and the Jewish captives to return and rebuild the temple. Darius I gave the second decree in 520 BC, which reconfirmed the first decree. In 458 BC, Artaxerxes Longimanus issued the third decree, which permitted Ezra to return and to be given safe passage and supplies in order to rebuild the temple. Finally, the fourth decree in 445 BC, also by Artaxerxes Longimanus, authorized Nehemiah to rebuild Jerusalem (Nehemiah 2:1–8).

There were to be "seven sets of seven" (i.e., forty-nine weeks), "plus sixty-two sets of seven" (i.e., 434 weeks), which equals 483 years. So from the time the command to rebuild Jerusalem was given until the time the

"Anointed One [Messiah] will be killed" would be 483 years of 360 days. *Daniel predicted the exact year that Jesus, the Messiah, would be crucified almost five hundred years before it occurred!*

Between the sixty-ninth and seventieth week, there is an interlude (not uncommon in prophecy, especially in Revelation). Theologians consider this interlude to be the period of the church. Jesus launched a new institution—the church (see Matthew 16:18). Paul described this as "God's mysterious plan" in Ephesians 3:1–6.

Daniel 9:26 states that "a ruler will arise whose armies will destroy the city and the Temple" (NLT). In AD 70, the Roman army, led by Titus, did exactly that. Titus prefigured the Antichrist to come, who will make a covenant with the Jews but break it and commit the "abomination of desolation" (Daniel 9:27 NLT). Jesus spoke of this in Matthew 25:15–22 and Matthew 24:15. Luke 21:24 speaks of the Jews being led away as captives into all the nations and Jerusalem being trampled by Gentiles "until the times of the Gentiles be fulfilled." Then God's dealings with the Jews will begin again, and the seventieth week will begin. Luke 21:25–27 describes the calamities that will occur.

The seventieth week is the tribulation period. Its purpose is to get Israel's attention in order to prepare the Jews to accept Christ's Second Advent (Second Coming, when Jesus returns to the earth). Jesus gave us a blueprint for His Second Coming. Many will be shocked when He returns but not true believers. They will recognize the signs Jesus laid out when He spoke to His disciples, as recorded by the apostle Matthew in his gospel:

1. False messiahs will come, claiming to be Jesus.
2. There will be wars and threats of wars.
3. Famines and earthquakes will take place in many parts of the world.
4. Christians will be hated, arrested, persecuted, and killed.
5. False prophets will deceive many people by performing signs and wonders.
6. Sin will be rampant everywhere.
7. The gospel will be preached throughout the whole earth.

"Then shall the end come" (Matthew 24:4–14).

Luke also recorded Jesus's comments on what would transpire prior to His Second Coming. It can be confusing because Jesus spoke of events that would occur in AD 70, as well as end-time events, which were blended together. Once again, although frustrating, this is typical of prophecy.

> And when you see Jerusalem surrounded by armies, then you will know that the time of its destruction has arrived. Then those in Judea must flee to the hills. Those in Jerusalem must get out, and those out in the country should not return to the city. For those will be days of God's vengeance, and the prophetic words of the Scriptures will be fulfilled. How terrible it will be for pregnant women and for nursing mothers in those days. For there will be disaster in the land and great anger against this people. They will be killed by the sword or sent away as captives to all the nations of the world. And Jerusalem will be trampled down by the Gentiles *until the period of the Gentiles comes to an end.* (Luke 21:20–24 NLT, emphasis mine)

In the New American Standard Bible, Luke 21:24 ends with "until the times of the Gentiles are fulfilled."

Essentially, almost all of what Jesus said occurred in AD 70 when the Roman army placed Jerusalem under siege and finally destroyed it. Titus did commit the "abomination of desolation" when he entered the temple in Jerusalem, ended the Jewish sacrifices, and sacrificed a pig (an unclean animal to the Jews) on the altar. Jesus had given signs of when to flee, and many Jewish Christians (messianics) did heed His warnings. However, not all that Jesus predicted occurred in AD 70. As I mentioned, Jesus spoke of both current events and end-time events. Let's look at the predictions that referred to the end time.

First, Jesus indicated there would come a time so terrible that it would be unlike anything the world had ever experienced, which he referred to as the "great tribulation."

> "For then shall be great tribulation, such as was not since the beginning of the world to this time, no, nor ever shall be.

And except those days should be shortened, there should no flesh be saved: but for the elect's sake those days shall be shortened." (Matthew 24:21–22)

Imagine a time so awful that unless God ends it early, no one will survive. Jesus said it will be the most terrible time in history, and nothing like it will ever occur again. We will see that the apostle John had more to say about this time in his book of Revelation. I am sure the Jews who were trapped inside Jerusalem during the Roman army's siege felt like they were in the great tribulation. Josephus, the Jewish historian, described in great detail how bad it was. People dying of hunger even ate their own children! But when we study John's description, the real great tribulation will be much worse.

Second, Jesus said that before the end comes, the gospel would be preached throughout the world. "And this gospel of the kingdom shall be preached in all the world for a witness unto all nations; and then shall the end come" (Matthew 24:14).

Some theologians teach that this already has occurred through the ministry of the apostle Paul. As proof of this, they quote Paul's comments to the Colossians, as follows:

> For the hope which is laid up for you in heaven, whereof ye heard before in the word of the truth of the gospel; Which is come unto you, as it is in *all the world*; and bringeth forth fruit, as it doth also in you, since the day ye heard of it, and knew the grace of God in truth ... If ye continue in the faith grounded and settled, and be not moved away from the hope of the gospel, which ye have heard, and *which was preached to every creature which is under heaven*; whereof I Paul am made a minister. (Colossians 1:5–6, 23, emphasis mine)

I see no evidence from Paul's writings that he felt as if he had reached everyone on earth with the gospel. The word *all* sometimes means all, but sometimes it's *all* in a more relative sense. I think Paul's intent was that he had made every effort to travel throughout the known world, setting up new churches everywhere he went. So to the extent possible, the gospel was delivered to all those places. Paul's hope was that those churches would reach "every creature which is under heaven" with the good news.

Third, the term "the times of the Gentiles" has caused significant confusion and has been interpreted in various ways. The basic concept is that with the Roman destruction of Jerusalem, a period called *the times of the Gentiles* began. As history records, the Jews were scattered throughout the world, and one Gentile empire after another subsequently controlled the land of Palestine until 1947, when Israel became a state. The question is, when did or does this period called the times of the Gentiles end? Some theologians believe it ended in 1947, when Israel was given their country back after almost nineteen hundred years. Others believe it ended during the Six-Day War in 1967, when the Israeli Defense Force occupied Jerusalem and, for the first time, captured the Western Wall and the Temple Mount. Jerusalem, however, remains a divided city, and Muslims are essentially in control of the Temple Mount, where the Dome of the Rock and Al-Aqsa Mosque are situated. So, in my mind, the times of the Gentiles may not have ended yet. This period may not end until the Jews possess the Temple Mount and can build the third temple. As you will see shortly, I believe this will occur as the result of the war of Gog and Magog.

Israel in End-Time Prophecy

Now let's look at what the Bible has to say about Israel in end-time prophecy. Two errors have crept into some spheres of Christian theology. I believe they were designed to diminish the role of Israel and actually have led to a spirit of anti-Semitism within the church. One is called *two-covenant (or dual-covenant) theology* and the other, *replacement theology*.

Two-covenant theology teaches that the old covenant was given to Israel, and the new covenant was given to the church. Hence, Jews are still saved by keeping the law of Moses (the old covenant), and Gentiles are saved by grace under the new covenant. The founders of two-covenant theology believed that Jesus's message was not for Jews but for Gentiles. This, however, cannot possibly be true—for many reasons. If you look at Paul's pattern for spreading the gospel wherever he went, he went first to the Jew and then to the Gentile, even though he was the apostle to the Gentiles.

Additionally, he made in clear to the church in Rome that Gentile believers are "grafted" into "Abraham's tree," or Israel (Romans 11:17–18). He pointed out to the Gentile Christians, "You are just a branch, not the root," the root being Israel (Romans 11:18b NLT).

Replacement theology teaches that the church has replaced Israel, and the church has become "spiritual Israel." Neither of these points could be farther from the truth. If you examine the covenants God made with Israel, starting with Abraham, you will find that each covenant is cloaked with the word "everlasting." When God says everlasting or forever, that is what He means. The apostle Paul dealt with this in his letter to the church at Rome. Just part of what he said is as follows:

> *I ask, then, has God rejected his own people, the nation of Israel? Of course not!* I myself am an Israelite, a descendant of Abraham and a member of the tribe of Benjamin. *No, God has not rejected his own people, whom he chose from the very beginning.*
>
> *Did God's people stumble and fall beyond recovery? Of course not!* They were disobedient, so God made salvation available to the Gentiles. But he wanted his own people to become jealous and claim it for themselves. But some of these branches from Abraham's tree—some of the people of Israel—have been broken off. And you Gentiles, who were branches from a wild olive tree, have been grafted in. So now you also receive the blessing God has promised Abraham and his children, sharing in the rich nourishment from the root of God's special olive tree. But you must not brag about being grafted in to replace the branches that were broken off. You are just a branch, not the root. You, by nature, were a branch cut from a wild olive tree. So if God was willing to do something contrary to nature by grafting you into his cultivated tree, he will be far more eager to graft the original branches back into the tree where they belong. I want you to understand this mystery, dear brothers and sisters, so that you will not feel proud about yourselves. Some of the people of Israel have hard hearts, but this will

last only until the full number of Gentiles comes to Christ. And so all Israel will be saved. As the Scriptures say,

"The one who rescues will come from Jerusalem,
and he will turn Israel away from ungodliness.
And this is my covenant with them,
that I will take away their sins."

Many of the people of Israel are now enemies of the Good News, and this benefits you Gentiles. Yet they are still the people he loves because he chose their ancestors Abraham, Isaac, and Jacob. *For God's gifts and his call can never be withdrawn [are irrevocable].* Once, you Gentiles were rebels against God, but when the people of Israel rebelled against him, God was merciful to you instead. Now they are the rebels, and God's mercy has come to you so that they, too, will share in God's mercy. For God has imprisoned everyone in disobedience so he could have mercy on everyone. (Romans 11:1–2, 11, 17–18, 24–32 NASB, emphasis mine)

In a sense, Paul was reiterating what God had said many years before through the prophet Jeremiah.

It is the Lord who provides the sun to light the day and the moon and stars to light the night, and who stirs the sea into roaring waves. His name is the Lord of Heaven's Armies, and this is what he says: *"I am as likely to reject my people Israel as I am to abolish the laws of nature!"*

This is what the Lord says: *"Just as the heavens cannot be measured and the foundations of the earth cannot be explored, so I will not consider casting them away for the evil they have done.* I, the Lord, have spoken!" (Jeremiah 31:35–37 NLT, emphasis mine)

Paul made it quite clear that the basis of the church is Israel—the "root." Gentiles have been grafted into it, and Jews who have accepted Christ as the Messiah have been regrafted in, after having been broken off. And both Paul and Jeremiah made it certain that God has not turned His back—nor will

He ever turn His back—on His chosen people, the Jews. People sometimes confuse the fact that God chose Israel as His "chosen people" with God playing favorites. But nothing could be farther from the truth. The Bible makes it quite clear that God is impartial. So what does it mean, then, for Israel to be the "chosen people"? I like how Rabbi Jonathan Bernis explained it in his book *A Rabbi Looks at the Last Days: Surprising Insights on Israel, the End Times and Popular Misconceptions*. He stated, "It is an issue of divine priority ... It is not about a priority based on loving one people more than another, but on God's divine order" (97).

Throughout the Old Testament, whenever judgment was prophesied, there was also the promise of restoration. A good example of this is in Ezekiel 36.

> Therefore say unto the house of Israel, thus saith the Lord God; "I do not this for your sakes, O house of Israel, but for mine holy name's sake, which ye have profaned among the heathen, whither ye went. And I will sanctify my great name, which was profaned among the heathen, which ye have profaned in the midst of them; and the heathen shall know that I am the Lord, saith the Lord God, when I shall be sanctified in you before their eyes. For I will take you from among the heathen, and gather you out of all countries, and will bring you into your own land." (Ezekiel 36:22–24)

God said He would bring the people of Israel back to their land from the four corners of the earth. He said He would do this not because they deserved it but to protect His holy name, the very name upon which they had brought shame. God would reveal His holiness through them, and as a result of this, the pagan nations would know that He is the one true God.

The restoration of the Jews will include not just being back in their own land again but also a cleansing and transformation of their hearts.

> Then will I sprinkle clean water upon you, and ye shall be clean: from all your filthiness, and from all your idols, will I cleanse you. A new heart also will I give you, and a new spirit will I put within you: and I will take away the stony

heart out of your flesh, and I will give you an heart of flesh.
And I will put my spirit within you, and cause you to walk in
my statutes, and ye shall keep my judgments, and do them.
(Ezekiel 36:25–27)

What a great day that will be! Finally, a day will come when His people will be cleansed of their sin, renewed from within, and given a "new heart," one that will be responsive to God. God will put His Spirit within them so they will obey His words. When will this occur? Paul made it clear that there had been a hardening of the hearts of the Jews but that it would last "only until the full number of the Gentiles comes to Christ." Then "all Israel will be saved."

I will explain more about this shortly, but first I want to consider another sign that the end is coming, which is the fulfillment of the prophecies concerning the return of the Jews to Israel.

Return of the Jews to the Promised Land

Isaiah prophesied,

For the Lord will have mercy on Jacob, and will yet choose
Israel, and set them in their own land: and the strangers
shall be joined with them, and they shall cleave to the house
of Jacob. And the people shall take them, and bring them
to their place: and the house of Israel shall possess them in
the land of the Lord for servants and handmaids: and they
shall take them captives, whose captives they were; and
they shall rule over their oppressors. (Isaiah 14:1–2)

Notice that something quite remarkable is within this prophecy. People from various nations will come and "cleave to the house of Jacob." In other words, they will come to live and unite with the Jews. How different than the spirit of anti-Semitism we see now throughout the world.

Similarly, the prophet Hosea prophesied,

Yet the number of the children of Israel shall be as the sand of the sea, which cannot be measured nor numbered; and it shall come to pass, that in the place where it was said unto them, "Ye are not my people," there it shall be said unto them, "Ye are the sons of the living God." Then shall the children of Judah and the children of Israel be gathered together, and appoint themselves one head, and they shall come up out of the land: for great shall be the day of Jezreel. (Hosea 1:10–11)

Jezreel means "God plants." So God is going to plant His people back in the land, and notice it will not just be Judah (southern kingdom) but also the ten tribes of Israel (northern kingdom). In 721 BC, the northern kingdom of Israel was carried off into captivity by Assyria. Then, in 586 BC, the southern kingdom of Judah was exiled to Babylon. Although seventy years later, those Jews exiled to Babylon were allowed to return, that was not the case for the northern kingdom of Israel, which was dispersed among its captors and never returned. They became known as the lost ten tribes. Hence, these prophecies that speak of both Judah and Israel returning to Israel were never fulfilled in OT times, and it was not possible until after the 1947 vote of the United Nations, which permitted the establishment of the modern state of Israel, which occurred in May 1948. This fulfilled the prophecy of Isaiah.

Who has ever seen anything as strange as this? Who ever heard of such a thing? Has a nation ever been born in a single day? Has a country ever come forth in a mere moment? But by the time Jerusalem's birth pains begin, her children will be born. (Isaiah 66:8 NLT)

Amos prophesied that once the Jews return, they won't go anywhere.

And I will bring again the captivity of my people of Israel, and they shall build the waste cities, and inhabit them; and they shall plant vineyards, and drink the wine thereof; they shall also make gardens, and eat the fruit of them. And I

> will plant them upon their land, and they shall no more be
> pulled up out of their land which I have given them, saith
> the Lord thy God. (Amos 9:14–15)

God promised to bring His people, who had been exiled to many foreign lands, back to the Promised Land, where they would rebuild their cities, plant vineyards, make and drink wine, and replant their gardens. And He intended to firmly plant them there so that they would never be taken captive again.

Ezekiel prophesied in chapters 36 and 37 that at a time when the Jews are "the property of many nations," they would return to the land of Israel. Ezekiel 37:1–14 describes the Valley of the Dry Bones, which comes to life, and God says, "And ye shall know that I am the Lord, when I have opened your graves, O my people, and brought you up out of your graves" (v. 13). What God meant by this was that He is going to bring them back into the land of Israel. This is followed by the prophecy of the Two Pieces of Wood, representing Israel (northern kingdom) and Judah (southern kingdom), which will be brought together once again as one piece of wood. When this happens, the people will be given a new tender and responsive heart and a new spirit. They will no longer worship idols. They will remember their past sins and despise themselves. God will cleanse them and make an everlasting covenant of peace and put His temple among them forever. As a result, all nations will know God is Lord by seeing His holiness through Israel.

As part of the fulfillment of these prophecies, the children of Israel were granted land in Palestine by the United Nations, and in 1948, the Jews started to officially return. After almost nineteen hundred years, the Jews were back in the Promised Land! This had never happened in human history. The purpose of exile is to disperse the people of a nation among the population of another nation or nations so that they cease to exist as a distinct people. But despite the repeated diasporas (dispersion and scattering) of the Jews and attempts to destroy them completely, as Hitler did in World War II, as well as others, God has preserved them. Now they are returning. Cities have been rebuilt and repopulated; the land has truly come back to life. Once again they are speaking Hebrew, which had become an almost dead language.

This, however, is just the start. The people have not yet repented of their sins. But there is a growing messianic movement (Jews who have accepted

Christ as the Messiah) in Israel. God is at work in Israel. He is preparing His people to receive Jesus when He returns. Jesus prophesied, "O Jerusalem, Jerusalem, thou that killest the prophets, and stonest them which are sent unto thee, how often would I have gathered thy children together, even as a hen gathereth her chickens under her wings, and ye would not! Behold, your house is left unto you desolate. For I say unto you, Ye shall not see me henceforth, till ye shall say, Blessed is he that cometh in the name of the Lord" (Matthew 23:37–39). Did you get that? The time is coming when Jesus will return, and when He does, the Jews will not only recognize who He is but also will be overjoyed and exclaim, "Blessed is he who comes in the name of the Lord." Throughout the centuries, God has longed to be accepted and received by His people. After a long period of rejection, finally this will happen. God is in the process of preparing the Jewish people to recognize and then receive Jesus, their Messiah.

The War of Gog and Magog

In Ezekiel 38 and 39, the prophet prophesied that there will be a great war between Gog and Magog and Israel. The countries that join together as allies to fight against Israel are listed very specifically: Magog, Rosh, Meshech, and Tubal (Russia and the former Soviet republics), Persia (Iran), Cush (Sudan, Ethiopia, and possibly Eritrea), Put (Libya, Algeria, and Tunisia), Gomer (Turkey and possibly Germany and Austria), Beth-togarmah (Turkey, Armenia, and the Turkic-speaking peoples of Asia Minor and central Asia), countries with mountainous borders with Israel (Syria, Lebanon, and northern Jordan), many peoples with you (possible additional Islamic allies), and Sheba and Dan (Saudi Arabia, Yemen, Oman, and the Gulf States).

Ezekiel states that Russia and its allies will attack Israel, and when all appears lost, God will display His power and holiness to the whole world with a "mighty shaking in the Land of Israel" with an earthquake, torrential rain with hailstones, fire and burning sulfur, and disease that will destroy the invading army. The loss of life will be enormous, and it will take seven months to bury the bodies—just imagine. This war likely will be broadcast worldwide, maybe in real time, on stations like CNN, the BBC, and many others. The entire world will marvel at what takes place, realizing that there is no way possible for Israel to be victorious except by God's divine intervention.

Isaiah also prophesied about a similar intervention of God: "But suddenly, your ruthless enemies will be crushed like the finest of dust. Your many attackers will be driven away like chaff before the wind. Suddenly, in an instant, I, the Lord of Heaven's Armies, will act for you with thunder and earthquake and great noise, with whirlwind and storm and consuming fire" (Isaiah 29:5–6 NLT).

A prophecy in Micah may be referring to this war as well: "The nations shall see and be confounded at all their might: they shall lay their hand upon their mouth, their ears shall be deaf" (Micah 7:16).

All the nations of the world are going to be shocked by what God does on behalf of Israel.

A fascinating read is *The Ezekiel Option* by Joel Rosenberg. He describes in detail how he thinks this might all play out. Although Russia supported the Muslims who fought against Israel in the War of Independence in 1947, the Six-Day War of 1967, and the War of Yom Kippur in 1973, they were not directly involved. However, Ezekiel makes it quite clear that Russia will spearhead the attack in the war of Gog and Magog, along with its allies. It is fascinating, as Rosenberg points out, that two countries fought in all three wars against Israel, but they are not mentioned as fighting in the war of Gog and Magog; namely, Egypt and Iraq. It may be that Egypt is not involved because in 1979, Egypt and Israel signed a formal peace treaty that has held up ever since.

For now, Iraq has been taken out of the picture due to the Iraq War, which began on March 20, 2003. A United States-led coalition, joined by the United Kingdom and several coalition allies, invaded Iraq and launched a shock-and-awe bombing campaign that ultimately toppled the government of Saddam Hussein. Unfortunately, a power vacuum subsequently developed. What followed was a prolonged insurgency against the United States and its coalition forces, due to widespread sectarian violence between Shias and Sunnis. President Barack Obama formally withdrew all combat troops from Iraq by December 2011.

As the result of God's obvious divine intervention, Israel will finally recognize their God and return to Him. God promises, "for I have poured out my spirit upon the house of Israel, saith the Lord God" (Ezekiel 39:29). The majority of Jews living in Israel today either are not religious or are nominally religious at best. They are Jewish, genealogically and culturally. As the prophets predicted long ago, God is drawing them back to the Promised Land. I believe that with God's dramatic and undeniable intervention in the war of Gog and Magog, many Jews will recognize their God and turn to Him.

Note: I don't think this necessarily means they will all become messianic believers. Some will, but this shift back to God and spiritual awakening is in preparation for their realization of who Jesus really is.

It is difficult to imagine the aftermath of this war. Russia and its Muslim allies will be so completely destroyed that their influence will be greatly reduced. One very disturbing fact, to me, is that there is no mention of the USA, currently Israel's number-one ally, coming to Israel's aid during this war. This may mean that for some reason the USA intentionally stays out of the conflict—maybe it will be because it has a president who is anti-Semitic, or maybe other countries will force the USA to stay out for political reasons. Another possibility is that by that time, the USA no longer will be a superpower because of unforeseen issues.

For whatever reason, however, God will use this abdication or pressured noninvolvement of the USA to display His glory. Everyone will realize that God protected and fought for Israel, and those familiar with biblical prophecy will realize that what Ezekiel predicted some twenty-five hundred years ago has come true! Not only that, but when Ezekiel made his predictions, Russia had no particular significance in the world. How could he possibly have known almost twenty-five hundred years ago that Russia would become a superpower? The answer is only by revelation from God.

Rebuilding of the Third Temple (Ezekiel's Temple)

Ezekiel 40–46 describes in great detail the temple that is to be built on Mount Moriah (the Temple Mount) in Jerusalem. As I have pointed out, currently the temple cannot be built because the Muslims have control of the Temple Mount, where the Dome of the Rock and the Al-Aqsa Mosque are situated. The Jews are very respectful of religious places and will not destroy these. My suspicion, however, is that God will take care of this problem with the great earthquake during the war of Gog and Magog; this is when I believe these structures will crumble. Ezekiel described the magnitude of this earthquake as follows:

> For in my jealousy and in the fire of my wrath have I spoken, surely in that day there shall be a great shaking in the land of Israel; so that the fishes of the sea, and the fowls of the heaven, and the beasts of the field, and all creeping things that creep upon the earth, and *all the men that are upon the face of the earth, shall shake at my presence,* and the mountains shall be thrown down, and the steep places shall fall, and every wall shall fall to the ground. (Ezekiel 38:19–20, emphasis mine)

Could this really mean that the entire earth will feel this shaking? If it is forceful enough for mountains to crumble, maybe. After the war, the radical Muslim influence that existed before the war will be seriously reduced, removing another significant obstacle to the temple's construction.

I first went to Israel several years ago, and I visited the Temple Institute, located in the Jewish Quarter of the Old City of Jerusalem. The institute's mission statement is clear: "The Temple Institute's ultimate goal is to see Israel rebuild the Holy Temple on Mount Moriah in Jerusalem, in accord with the Biblical commandments." While there, I saw an exact replica of the third temple (Ezekiel's temple) that is to be built. Jewish craftsman have been preparing the sacred temple vessels and priestly garments necessary to reestablish the sacrifices in the temple. Since AD 70, when the Romans destroyed the temple, the Jews have had no way for their sins to be forgiven because the sacrifices ceased. Therefore, the Orthodox Jews, since they reject Jesus as the Messiah, are eager to reinstitute the sacrificial system.

The prophet Haggai made an interesting prophecy:

> For thus saith the Lord of hosts; Yet once, it is a little while, and I will shake the heavens, and the earth, and the sea, and the dry land; And I will shake all nations, and the desire of all nations shall come: and I will fill this house with glory,

saith the Lord of hosts. The silver is mine, and the gold is
mine, saith the Lord of hosts. The glory of this latter house
shall be greater than of the former, saith the Lord of hosts:
and in this place will I give peace, saith the Lord of hosts.
(Haggai 2:6–9 NLT)

There it is again—a great shaking! God is speaking here through Haggai
of the future glory of the temple (referred to as the "latter house"), which
is going to be even greater than in the past. That is saying a lot because the
first temple was incredible at the time of Solomon, and Herod the Great
expanded the Temple Mount and made the whole area of the second temple
even more magnificent. Some of this prophecy was certainly fulfilled when
the temple was rebuilt after the Jews returned from Babylon and later, when
Herod did his elaborate expansion project of the Temple Mount.

There are good reasons, however, to see a future fulfillment as well. The
"desire of all nations" would refer to Jesus, the Messiah. He came into the
temple when He rode into Jerusalem through the Eastern Gate on a donkey
on Palm Sunday. However, it also will occur at His second Coming, when
He enters the third temple. Some versions of the Bible translate *desire* as
treasures. If this is correct, then this may refer to the wealth that the nations
bring to the third temple during the millennium, as prophesied in Isaiah:
"Your eyes will shine, and your heart will thrill with joy, for merchants from
around the world will come to you. They will bring you the wealth of many
lands" (Isaiah 60:5 NLT).

This shaking of the heavens and earth was quoted in the book of Hebrews
12:26–27 and clearly refers to a future event: "Whose voice then shook the
earth: but now he hath promised, saying, 'Yet once more I shake not the
earth only, but also heaven.' And this word, 'Yet once more,' signifieth the
removing of those things that are shaken, as of things that are made, that
those things which cannot be shaken may remain."

So God is going to "shake" His creation, and only unshakable things
will remain. The obvious implication from these verses is that in the end,
the earth will crumble and disappear, but God's kingdom will last forever.

Once the third temple is built, the stage will be set for the emergence
of the Antichrist.

Daniel's Seventieth Week—the Tribulation

In Revelation 4–19, we see God's judgment upon the world preceding Christ's return and His earthly reign. This is called the *tribulation* period. A man called the Antichrist will make a covenant with Israel (Revelation 9:26), and at the midpoint of the seven-year tribulation period, he will break that covenant. He will end Jewish sacrifices and commit the *abomination of desolation* in the temple. (Daniel 11:31; 12:11; Matthew 24:15–21; Mark 13:14). This abomination of desolation was prefigured by Antiochus Ephiphanes, the Seleucid king who ruled Palestine. In 168/167 BC, in order to suppress Jewish rebellion, his army entered the temple, brought an end to the sacrifices, set up an altar to the god Zeus, and offered a pig as a sacrifice. This defilement of the holy place was an abomination that caused desolation. As I previously explained, the Roman commander Titus and his forces did a similar thing in AD 70, which was also a prefigurement of what the Antichrist will one day do. After the Antichrist commits this defiling act, he will then wage war against God's people (Revelation 13:4–7).

A description of the Antichrist was revealed to Daniel:

> A king of fierce countenance, and understanding dark sentences, shall stand up. And his power shall be mighty, but not by his own power: and he shall destroy wonderfully, and shall prosper, and practise, and shall destroy the mighty and the holy people. And through his policy also he shall cause craft to prosper in his hand; and he shall magnify himself in his heart, and by peace shall destroy many: he shall also stand up against the Prince of princes; but he shall be broken without hand. (Daniel 8:23–25)

This person will be very charismatic and persuasive but also fierce, a master of intrigue and deception, crafty, incredibly powerful, arrogant, and prideful. He will be possessed with demonic power such that when he is destroyed, it will not be by human power but by God Himself. In every way, he is a counterfeit of Jesus, the real Christ. However, his traits are diametrically opposed to Jesus's traits. Jesus was humble, but the Antichrist will be proud and arrogant. Jesus came with love and compassion for people, but the Antichrist will deceive and control people, eventually forcing them to worship him. Jesus's power came from God, but the Antichrist's power will come from Satan.

We learn more about this person who is represented as a beast in Revelation 13, who is a blasphemer of God. Satan, described as the dragon, gives the Antichrist "his power, and his seat (throne), and great authority" (Revelation 13:2). At some point the Antichrist will receive some form of fatal wound, but he won't die. He will recover, which will represent a false resurrection. As a result, the whole world will be amazed. The world will give allegiance to the Antichrist and worship him. He will literally deceive the entire world, except for believers. He will actually make a covenant of peace with Israel, but at the midpoint of the tribulation, he will break this covenant and turn on Israel. He will blaspheme God for three and a half years and will be allowed "to make war with the saints, and to overcome them" (Revelation 13:7). Satan will try to destroy Jews and believers, but God will use this time of testing to refine His people. This beast represents himself as God, but it's all a deception that will come to an end when God deals with him.

The judgments of the tribulation will be upon unbelievers. People will see and experience the bitter alternative to the lordship of Jesus Christ. "That they all might be damned who believed not the truth, but had pleasure in unrighteousness" (2 Thessalonians 2:12). Those who choose not to believe the truth and enjoy doing evil will be condemned. They essentially will condemn themselves by their sinful practices.

The judgments doled out during the tribulation are not random but purposeful. They are designed to accomplish three things:

1. Bring an end to wickedness on the earth. Isaiah prophesied this: "See, the day of the Lord is coming— a cruel day, with wrath and fierce anger to make the land desolate and destroy the sinners within it" (Isaiah 13:9).
2. Bring a worldwide revival. God's desire is that all would be saved.
3. Break the stubborn will of Israel. Ezekiel prophesied,
   As I live, saith the Lord God, surely with a mighty hand, and with a stretched out arm, and with fury poured out, will I rule over you: And I will bring you out from the people, and will gather you out of the countries wherein ye are scattered, with a mighty hand, and

with a stretched out arm, and with fury poured out. And I will bring you into the wilderness of the people, and there will I plead with you face to face. Like as I pleaded with your fathers in the wilderness of the land of Egypt, so will I plead with you, saith the Lord God. And I will cause you to pass under the rod, and I will bring you into the bond of the covenant. (Ezekiel 20:33–37)

God intends to bring His people back from where they have been scattered throughout the earth to the Promised Land. He then will deal with them, just like He did when He brought them out of Egypt. He will remind them of all the terms of the covenant He made with them and hold them accountable to those terms.

The Apocalypse

The word *apocalypse* comes from a Greek word which means *an uncovering*. The book of Revelation, also called John's Apocalypse, is God's revelation (uncovering) of what was previously hidden or unknown concerning the end of the age and how God will triumph over Satan, winning the final age-old battle of good versus evil.

In the first chapter of Revelation, John explained what led him to write the book, and then in the next two chapters, Jesus gave instructions to seven specific churches in Asia Minor. The seven churches are believed to be archetypes or patterns. Each possessed characteristics that are representative of all types of churches throughout time. Hence, any church, even today, can read these instructions and then take a look in the mirror to evaluate the good, bad, and ugly within that church.

Starting in Revelation 4, everything changes. John is caught up to heaven and begins the roller coaster ride of his life! I want to summarize in some detail what is described in Revelation 4–19. In order to understand this section best, it would be helpful if you read the corresponding chapters in your Bible as I go chapter by chapter. That way, you will get the full picture of what is going on. Chapters 4 through 19 deal with the period called the tribulation. Jesus called this "the beginning of sorrows" (Matthew 24:8) and said it would get progressively worse until it becomes the "great tribulation."

Jesus compared the tribulation to a woman's labor pains. As labor progresses, labor pains become more intense and more frequent. Hence, during the tribulation, the judgments of God will become progressively worse and more intense. Some terrible things are about to happen on earth, and most people will not be prepared. In fact, things will get so bad at the end that no one will be able to survive, and they only survive because God "for the elect's sake those days shall be shortened" (Matthew 24:22).

It will be this way because God's judgments will be in proportion to man's wickedness. The apostle Paul said, "That they all might be damned who believed not the truth, but had pleasure in unrighteousness" (2 Thessalonians 2:12). In other words, men will enjoy sinning and prefer it over the truth. Although man loves to sin, sin brings about man's self-destruction. God's judgment of sin ends this self-destruction. Perhaps it is only the judgment of God, due to His love and grace, that intervenes to prevent man from totally destroying himself. When I was growing up, this was a major concern during the Cold War. And as I write this, these concerns have been renewed by North Korea's possession of nuclear weapons.

But remember, as terrible as all this will be, our God is not vindictive or capricious. He is a God of love. His judgments are levied, hoping men will turn from their sin and repent. Also remember that God has the end in sight. At the end of labor, a woman gives birth to a beautiful baby. She is overjoyed and no longer thinks about the pain of her labor. At the end of the tribulation, Jesus will defeat evil and establish His millennial kingdom on earth. What every man's heart throughout the ages has longed for will come when the Prince of Peace finally brings peace and justice to earth.

Despite what's coming, Jesus assured us, "See that ye be not troubled" (Matthew 24:6). God will be in control. Although the world will be totally freaked out by what's going on around them, we will get it. We will recognize the signs Jesus predicted—the signs of His imminent return!

Revelation 4—John sees God's throne in heaven from where the judgment comes.

There are not many places in scripture where we get a direct look into heaven. If you are interested, I suggest you also read Revelation 1:9–20, Isaiah 6:1–10, Ezekiel 1:1–28 and 10:1–22, and Daniel 7:9–10. It's incredible how similar these visions are.

Revelation 5—God is sitting on His throne, holding a scroll with seven seals. Jesus, the Lamb of God, the Lion of the tribe of Judah, is the only one worthy to remove the seals. He steps forward and takes the scroll.

Have you ever wondered if your prayers are important and whether they have any effect? James, the brother of Jesus, said, "The effectual fervent prayer of a righteous man availeth much" (James 5:16). He was encouraging each of us to pray earnestly because our prayers possess great power and will produce wonderful results. We see some of those results here in Revelation 5. John saw twenty-four elders sitting on thrones surrounding God the Father, who was sitting on His throne. After Jesus took the scroll, the twenty-four elders fell down to worship Jesus, the Lamb of God. Each elder had a gold bowl filled with incense, "which are the prayers of saints" (Revelation 5:8). Do you realize this? Some of your prayers may be stored in gold bowls in heaven right now. At the right time, they are poured out before your heavenly Father, and He will answer your prayers.

John sees millions of angels around God's throne, which form a "mighty chorus" that sings, "Worthy is the Lamb that was slain to receive power, and riches, and wisdom, and strength, and honour, and glory, and blessing" (Revelation 5:12). I can't begin to imagine what this will sound like. My son and I had the privilege of attending Super Bowl XX, which was played on January 26, 1986, in the Louisiana Superdome in New Orleans. We were Chicago Bears fans, and let me tell you, there was some shouting going on that day inside the dome! It was loud, with over eighty thousand cheering fans. But millions of angels singing at the top of their voices—how loud will that be?

The Seven Seal Judgments

The seven seal judgments will upset every aspect of men's lives. The shaking that is about to occur is reminiscent of Hebrews 12:26–27, which says, "Whose voice then shook the earth: but now he hath promised, saying, Yet once more I shake not the earth only, but also heaven. And this word, Yet once more, signifieth the removing of those things that are shaken, as of things that are made, that those things which cannot be shaken may remain."

The repeated shaking of the heavens and the earth that will occur first with the seven seal judgments and then with the trumpet and vial judgments will leave only God's unshakable kingdom.

Revelation 6—Seals 1 through 4 represent the Four Horsemen of the Apocalypse.

Seal 1: White horse; conquest.

Seal 2: Red horse; war and conflict.

Seal 3: Black horse; scarcity and inequity (famine).

Seal 4: Pale horse; death by sword, famine, plague, and wild beasts.

Seal 5: Cry of the martyrs; they cry out for vengeance and justice.

Seal 6: Cosmic disruption with terror destroys one-quarter of the earth's population. This is reminiscent of the plague epidemic (also known as the Black Death) that swept through Eurasia and Europe in the fourteenth century. It was a disease caused by the bacterium Yersinia pestis, which lived in black rats. The rats served as the hosts, and the bacterium was spread to humans by rat fleas. The rats lived on merchant ships, which transported them and the disease from one country to the next. From 1346 to 1353, so many people died from the plague that the world's population was reduced by over 25 percent. Imagine if the world's population at the time of the sixth seal judgment is, say, eight billion. That means two billion people will die.

John sees an altar in heaven with the souls of those who had been martyred underneath it. They shout to God, "How long, O Lord, holy and true, dost thou not judge and avenge our blood on them that dwell on the earth?" (Revelation 6:10). They are each given a white robe to wear and told to wait and rest a "little" longer until they are joined by the rest of the martyrs who are coming. They echo the age-old human cry for justice. The intense persecution will purify the church to an extent like never before. The bride of Christ is being prepared so she will be "without spot or wrinkle" (Ephesians 5:27). Its intensity will also cause Christians to pray more fervently and frequently. God will hear the cries (prayers) of His people and respond. However, the oppression will also cause a falling away, as Paul warned the church at Thessalonica. "Let no man deceive you by any means: for that day [Christ's return] shall not come, except there come a falling away first" (2 Thessalonians 2:3).

Revelation 7—The 144,000 chosen Jewish messianic believers, protectively sealed throughout the tribulation, are the beginning of the salvation of Israel.

The great multitude; saints before the throne worshiping God, defined as, "These are they which came out of great tribulation, and have washed their robes, and made them white in the blood of the Lamb" (Revelation 7:14). Many are saved in the midst of judgment (perhaps the result of the evangelism of the 144,000).

Revelation 8—Silence in heaven for half an hour (a pause for emphasis). I did a study on silence in the Bible. It is not uncommon for a period of silence to precede something big that God is about to do.

Seal 7: Seven angels given seven trumpets; the prayers of the saints ascend to heaven prior to these judgments.

The Seven Trumpet Judgments

God proclaims His Lordship through agonizing disruption:

Trumpet 1: Plague on vegetation; hail and fire with blood.

Trumpet 2: Plague on the sea; sea turns to blood and one-third of the creatures die.

Trumpet 3: Plague on fresh waters; a star like a torch falls into the rivers and springs and one-third become bitter; men die.

Trumpet 4: Plague on the heavens and darkness on the earth; an angel cries out, "Woe, woe, woe" because of the remaining three trumpet judgments, which are called the three woes.

We recently had a solar eclipse that was observed in the central United States. I spoke with people who witnessed it, and they described the moment of "totality" as an incredible experience; some actually cried. But it lasted only a very short time. The darkness described here in the fourth trumpet judgment will be terrifying. People likely will cry but for a very different reason.

Revelation 9

Trumpet 5 (first woe): Demonic locusts come from the bottomless pit and attack men (but not plants and not those with the seal of God) in order to bring repentance. This is the discipline of God. Perhaps these are wicked demons who have always desired to possess bodies, whose king is Abaddon (Satan).

Trumpet 6: Four angels who kill one-third of mankind (second woe);

these angels lead an army of two hundred million horsemen. The horses breathe out fire, smoke, and brimstone. How could an army of two hundred million kill two billion people? We do not know if these are men, demons, or creatures with artificial intelligence. Yet despite all of this, men still don't repent!

These plagues sound very much like the judgment predicted by Isaiah.

> The earth mourneth and fadeth away, the world languisheth and fadeth away, the haughty people of the earth do languish. The earth also is defiled under the inhabitants thereof; because they have transgressed the laws, changed the ordinance, broken the everlasting covenant. Therefore hath the curse devoured the earth, and they that dwell therein are desolate: therefore the inhabitants of the earth are burned, and few men left. (Isaiah 24:4–6)

As a result of man's sin and rebellion against God, a curse will devour the earth. Most frightening of all is that only a "few men" will remain.

Some of this may have been prefigured by the Babylonian captivity, but what Isaiah says later in this chapter refers to the end time.

> Terror and traps and snares will be your lot, you people of the earth. Those who flee in terror will fall into a trap, and those who escape the trap will be caught in a snare.
>
> Destruction falls like rain from the heavens; the foundations of the earth shake. The earth has broken up. It has utterly collapsed; it is violently shaken. The earth staggers like a drunk. It trembles like a tent in a storm. It falls and will not rise again, for the guilt of its rebellion is very heavy. In that day the Lord will punish the gods in the heavens and the proud rulers of the nations on earth. They will be rounded up and put in prison. They will be shut up in prison and will finally be punished. (Isaiah 24:17–22 NLT)

Revelation 10—Interlude; this again is God's mercy giving people the opportunity to repent.

A mighty angel comes down from heaven and cries out, "Seven thunders!" He stands with one foot on the sea and one foot on the land, with a little book (scroll) in his hand. The angel then speaks: "No more delay. When the seventh angel blows his trumpet, God's mysterious plan will be fulfilled" (Revelation 10:7 NLT). John was not allowed to reveal what the seven thunders spoke; he was told to seal it up.

John was then told to eat the little scroll and prophecy. This is reminiscent of Ezekiel 3:1–3. We are not told what this mysterious plan is, but it is now coming to an end—the resolution of all things and the summing up of all things in Christ (Ephesians 1:10).

Revelation 11—John is told to measure the temple.

Presumably this is the third temple in Jerusalem, built to fulfill Daniel's prophecy regarding the abomination of desolation (Daniel 9:27; 11:31; 12:11; Matthew 24:15–16; 2 Thessalonians 2:3–4). The act of measuring is symbolic, implying that God is in charge. John is told, "But the court which is without the temple leave out, and measure it not; for it is given unto the Gentiles: and the holy city shall they tread under foot forty and two months." In other words this three-and-a-half-year period is probably when the Antichrist pours out his fury on the people of Israel in the second half of the tribulation.

Two witnesses, who are dressed in burlap, will prophesy for three and a half years and have incredible power. Zechariah may have made reference to these two witnesses (Zechariah 4:14). They will have the power to bring about the same kind of plagues that Moses did in Egypt (Exodus 7–10) and stop rain from falling, as Elijah did (1 Kings 17:1). Then the Beast will kill them, but after three and half days they will come to life and ascend to heaven. This will be followed by a terrible earthquake.

Trumpet 7 (third woe): There is great joy in heaven with worship of God. "The kingdoms of this world are become the kingdoms of our Lord, and of his Christ; and he shall reign for ever and ever" (Revelation 11:15). The temple of God is opened, followed by an earthquake and a terrible hailstorm.

Revelation 12—A pregnant woman clothed with the sun and a crown with twelve stars gives birth to a son. This woman has been interpreted to be Mary, the church, and/or Israel.

A large red dragon with seven heads, ten horns, and seven crowns sweeps away one-third of the stars in the sky and throws them to earth. He prepares to devour the child, but God snatches the child up to His throne.

There is war in heaven. Satan and his angels are cast out and thrown down to earth at the midpoint of the tribulation. Satan will be denied access to heaven. His days of accusing the saints will be over. So he will turn his attention to earth. As a result, things will get much worse on earth, and the period of the great tribulation (the last half of the seven-year tribulation period) will begin. John stated, "Therefore, rejoice, O heavens! And you who live in the heavens, rejoice! But terror will come on the earth and the sea, for the devil has come down to you in great anger, knowing that he has little time" (Revelation 12:12 NLT).

Imagine—the devil will not only be angry but furious. He won't be happy knowing his time is almost over. So he will cause as much destruction as possible in the time he has left.

The dragon pursues the woman, but God protects her in a prepared place in the wilderness. So Satan pursues her children. Jesus warned of this (Matthew 24:15–22), telling the Jews to flee to the wilderness. The Jews who recognized the signs of which Jesus spoke in AD 70 also fled. The same will be true again. God will protect them.

Revelation 13—Beast with seven heads, ten horns, and ten crowns is the Antichrist (Daniel 7:7). This satanic messiah (1 John 2:18) comes out of the sea (evil chaos); one head is fatally wounded but heals (a false resurrection). As a result, the world marvels and gives allegiance to the Beast. The Beast is given authority for three and a half years, wages war against God's people (persecution), and rules over the nations.

But the apostle Peter assures us that this time of trials will have beneficial results: "That the trial of your faith, being much more precious than of gold that perisheth, though it be tried with fire, might be found unto praise and honour and glory at the appearing of Jesus Christ" (1 Peter 1:7). Trials produce genuine faith, and when Jesus returns, those who have persevered will be praised, honored, and given glory. Sounds like the adulation given the athletes who win the Super Bowl. However, winning the Super Bowl will be nothing compared to this.

The Antichrist will become the world leader.

Another beast comes up from the earth (false prophet) with two horns. He requires all people to worship the Beast and performs astounding miracles. Jesus predicted false prophets (Matthew 24:24). This false prophet is Satan's counterfeit Holy Spirit. Paul predicted the Antichrist would come with power, signs, and lying wonders (2 Thessalonians 2:9). A golden statue of the Antichrist is erected by an apostate angel; it speaks! Everyone is required to take the mark of the Beast (imitating God's mark, His seal on the saints).

The dragon, Beast, and false prophet are the unholy trinity and will impersonate the one true and only triune God.

Revelation 14—The Lamb is standing with 144,000 saints on Mount Zion, who sing a "new song" and follow the Lamb wherever He goes. They are those who were purchased from among the people of the earth as a special offering (first fruits) to God and the Lamb. I believe these were the messianics sealed in Revelation 7, who now emerge victorious with Jesus.

First angel flies in the sky and proclaims the good news to all people who belong to this world.

Second angel shouts, "Babylon is fallen" (Revelation 14:8).

Third angel shouts, "If any man worship the beast and his image, and receive his mark in his forehead, or in his hand, the same shall drink of the wine of the wrath of God, which is poured out without mixture into the cup of his indignation; and he shall be tormented with fire and brimstone in the presence of the holy angels, and in the presence of the Lamb" (Revelation 14:9–10). God's people must endure persecution, but we are told, "Blessed are those who die in the Lord from now on. Yes, says the Spirit, they are blessed indeed, for they will rest from their hard work; for their good deeds follow them!" (Revelation 14:13 NLT).

It's not very comforting to think about the possibility of undergoing persecution. It's natural to think, *I'm not very brave. I don't know if I could do it.* Look what the apostle Peter had to say to Jewish Christians in the early church who were scattered due to persecution:

> Blessed be the God and Father of our Lord Jesus Christ, who according to His abundant mercy has begotten us again to a living hope through the resurrection of Jesus Christ from the dead, to an inheritance incorruptible and undefiled and that does not fade away, reserved in heaven for you, who are kept by the power of God through faith

for salvation ready to be revealed in the last time. (1 Peter 1:3–5)

Peter assured those who were undergoing persecution that their hope was in God, who had an incredible inheritance awaiting them on their arrival in heaven, whether by natural causes or martyrdom. He also assured them that they were being "kept by the power of God." There is no greater power than God's power! We simply need to place our faith, our trust, in God. When our strength runs out, His will intervene.

The writer of the book of Hebrews states, "Therefore He is also able to save to the uttermost those who come to God through Him, since He always lives to make intercession for them" (Hebrews 7:25). Do you realize that if you believe in who the Bible says Jesus is, and you have made Him the Lord of your life, then He constantly intercedes on your behalf? One of the reasons He has been interceding for us is because Satan constantly has been accusing us (Revelation 12:10). Jesus is not just sitting in heaven at the right hand of His Father, watching. He has been very busy praying on our behalf. You would think it would have been enough for Him to die for each of us, but no; now He continues to intercede for us so that we will be kept by God's power.

Similarly, prior to His Crucifixion, Jesus prayed for His disciples. He knew the world would persecute them in the same way the world had persecuted Him. Listen to His prayer, His intercession, on their behalf:

> Now I am no longer in the world, but these are in the world, and I come to You. Holy Father, keep through Your name those whom You have given Me, that they may be one as We are. While I was with them in the world, *I kept them in Your name.* Those whom You gave Me I have kept; and none of them is lost except the son of perdition, that the Scripture might be fulfilled. But now I come to You, and these things I speak in the world, that they may have My joy fulfilled in themselves. I have given them Your word; and the world has hated them because they are not of the world, just as I am not of the world. *I do not pray that You should take them out*

of the world, but that You should keep them from the evil one.
(John 17:11–15, emphasis added)

The bottom line is that we have Jesus, our high priest, in heaven, constantly praying on our behalf. He is not only the Lamb of God who died for us, but He is also our Savior and Intercessor.

The Second Coming of Jesus Christ (He Comes as the Righteous Judge)

The Son of Man comes on a white cloud (Second Coming) with a gold crown and sharp sickle.

An angel shouts, "Swing the sickle" (Revelation 14:15).

Two more angels: One, with a sharp sickle, swings and loads grapes into the winepress of God's wrath. The heel of His omnipotence crushes them. Blood flows 180 miles, as high as a horse's bridle. One has the power to destroy by fire from the altar in heaven.

When Jesus Christ returns he will slay the Antichrist with the breath of His mouth and destroy him by the splendor of His coming. The apostle Paul spoke of this:

> Concerning the coming of our Lord Jesus Christ and our being gathered to him, we ask you, brothers and sisters, not to become easily unsettled or alarmed by the teaching allegedly from us—whether by a prophecy or by word of mouth or by letter—asserting that the *day of the Lord* has already come. Don't let anyone deceive you in any way, for that day will not come until the rebellion occurs and the *man of lawlessness* (Antichrist) is revealed, the man doomed to destruction. He will oppose and will exalt himself over everything that is called God or is worshiped, so that he sets himself up in God's temple, proclaiming himself to be God. Don't you remember that when I was with you I used to tell you these things? And now you know what is holding him back, so that he may be revealed at the proper

time. For the secret power of lawlessness is already at work; but the one who now holds it back will continue to do so till he is taken out of the way. And then the lawless one will be revealed, *whom the Lord Jesus will overthrow with the breath of his mouth and destroy by the splendor of his coming*. (2 Thessalonians 2:1–8 NIV, emphasis added)

The prophet Zechariah described Jesus's Second Coming this way:

Then shall the Lord go forth, and fight against those nations, as when he fought in the day of battle. And his feet shall stand in that day upon the mount of Olives, which is before Jerusalem on the east, and the mount of Olives shall cleave in the midst thereof toward the east and toward the west, and there shall be a very great valley; and half of the mountain shall remove toward the north, and half of it toward the south. And ye shall flee to the valley of the mountains; for the valley of the mountains shall reach unto Azal: yea, ye shall flee, like as ye fled from before the earthquake in the days of Uzziah king of Judah: and the Lord my God shall come, and all the saints with thee. (Zechariah 14:3–5)

When Jesus returns, He will stand on the Mount of Olives, prepared to do battle with those who have rejected Him and persecuted His people. When He returns, He will bring all the saints with Him.

Malachi described the event like this: "But who may abide the day of his coming? and who shall stand when he appeareth? for he is like a refiner's fire, and like fullers' soap" (Malachi 3:2).

When Jesus returns, no one will be able to stand up and face Him. He is described as a refiner's blazing fire and like strong bleach.

The prophet Joel prophesied,

Multitudes, multitudes in the valley of decision: for the day of the Lord is near in the valley of decision. The sun and the moon shall be darkened, and the stars shall withdraw their shining. The Lord also shall roar out of Zion, and utter his voice from Jerusalem; and the heavens and the earth shall shake: but the Lord will be the hope of his people, and the strength of the children of Israel. So shall ye know that I am the Lord your God dwelling in Zion, my holy mountain: then shall Jerusalem be holy, and there shall no strangers pass through her any more. (Joel 3:14–17)

When Jesus returns, He will be both the hope and the fortress for the Jews. They will recognize Jesus is the Messiah living in Jerusalem. Jerusalem will be "holy," and foreign armies will never rule over her again.

Revelation 15—a prelude to the seven bowl judgments

A sign in heaven is seven angels with the seven last plagues to complete the wrath of God (Leviticus 26:21). Although some will have turned to God due to the seal and trumpet judgments, many will still shake their fists at God and blaspheme. Hence, they will receive the seven bowl (vial) judgments, or the complete wrath of God. The faith of believers during the tribulation will stand in marked contrast to the fear of unbelievers.

John sees a sea of glass, with those who have victory over the beast holding harps—these are the tribulation martyrs of Revelation 7:9–17 (the early church consistently described the day of martyrdom as "a day of victory"), who sing the "song of Moses" or "song of the Lamb" (old covenant/ new covenant).

The seven angels are given seven bowls. They come from the presence of God. A cloud of smoke fills the temple (this is consistent with the Shekinah glory that filled the earthly tabernacle—Exodus 40:34–35).

Revelation 16

The seven bowl judgments (third woe): These are designed to bring repentance to all those who bear the mark of the Beast.

The first four bowl judgments are against man and nature:

- *First bowl*—Malignant sores.
- *Second bowl*—Sea becomes like blood, and everything dies.
- *Third bowl*—Rivers and springs become blood. Those who shed blood now have to drink it. They refused living water, so now they must drink the water of death.

- *Fourth bowl*—Sun scorches everyone with fire.

The last three bowl judgments are against the Beast and his government:

- *Fifth bowl*—The throne of the Beast and his kingdom are plunged into darkness (this is consistent with Exodus 10:21–22), a preview of hell itself. Jesus described it as "outer darkness" (Matthew 25:30).
- *Sixth bowl*—Euphrates River dries up, which opens the way for the kings of the east (e.g., China, India, Japan). Three evil spirits come from the mouth of the dragon, the Antichrist, and the false prophet. They go out and work miracles and gather the rulers of the world for battle against God to the place called Armageddon (in Hebrew, Har Megiddo). Mount Megiddo is actually only a tel. The plain of Megiddo is approximately sixty miles north of Jerusalem. This battle is "that great day of God Almighty."

This will be Satan's last-ditch effort to retain control of the earth prior to Jesus's return. With the fall in the garden of Eden, man relinquished his authority over the earth to Satan. That's why Jesus referred to Satan as "the prince [ruler] of this world" (John 12:31; 14:30; 16:11), and the apostle Paul called him "the god of this world" (2 Corinthians 4:4) and "the prince of the power of the air" (Ephesians 2:2).

When Satan tempted Jesus in the wilderness, he offered to give him his authority over "all the kingdoms of the world." It would not have been much of a temptation if Satan had no authority to give (Luke 4:5–7). Throughout history Satan has been on a relentless campaign to thwart God's plans. He tried repeatedly to annihilate the Jews, God's chosen people, through whom the promised Messiah would come. When that didn't work, he tried to kill the Messiah after He was born. Again, he failed. He did have Jesus killed at the Crucifixion, but he never counted on the resurrection. Foiled again! Since Jesus's ascension, he has continued his persecution of both Jews and Christians. He has tried to annihilate the Jews many times—the Holocaust being just one example.

Satan managed to convince Adam and Eve that God was somehow holding out on them. This led to their sin. Satan has been spinning that same lie ever since, and men keep falling for it. So, in this Battle of Armageddon, Satan will lead all those he has deceived against God.

The prophet Joel described this battle:

For, behold, in those days, and in that time, when I shall bring again the captivity of Judah and Jerusalem, I will also gather all nations, and will bring them down into the valley of Jehoshaphat, and will plead with them there for my people and for my heritage Israel, whom they have scattered among the nations, and parted my land. Let the heathen be wakened, and come up to the valley of Jehoshaphat: for there will I sit to judge all the heathen round about. Put ye in the sickle, for the harvest is ripe: come, get you down; for the press is full, the fats overflow; for their wickedness is great. (Joel 3:1–2, 12–13)

When the evil nations of the world come to do battle against God, God will judge them. There is no valley in Israel named the valley of Jehoshaphat. The name is symbolic, meaning the judgment of God. God is going to judge all the nations of the earth for how they mistreated His people, both the Jews and Christians. Many people ask, "How can God allow or permit injustice and suffering in the world?" Well, our God promises that one day He will come and make everything right. No one will have gotten away with anything. Everyone will be called into account. The only reason He delays is so that all who are going to be saved will be saved.

- *Seventh bowl*—God shouts, "It is finished!" Thunder, lightning, and the worst earthquake ever occurs. Babylon is split in three. Cities of the nations fall in rubble. Every island disappears, and mountains disappear. Seventy-five-pound hailstones fall. (Hail is a tool of judgment; see Exodus 9:24; 38:22; Joshua 10:11; Isaiah 28:2.) "It is done!" Jesus uttered these same words, "It is done!" or "It is finished!" on the cross immediately before He died (John 18:30). He came the first time as the "suffering servant," and He will come the second time as the "King of Glory"—the righteous judge. In both cases, He completes what He comes to do.

Revelation 17—the fall of the great city of Babylon (or the "Great Prostitute")

The fall of Babylon (Revelation 16:19; 14:8) will now be detailed.

Religious Babylon, who corrupted the earth with immorality and who is drunk with the blood of the martyrs of Jesus, comes riding on the Beast (Antichrist). Contrast the woman of Revelation 12 (Israel, God's people) with this harlot (idolatrous, false religion). In contrast to the bride of Christ, she is Satan's counterfeit bride. She embodies Satan's ecumenical movement, which is the world's religious system.

The Beast (Antichrist) has seven heads representing seven mountains (or kings_:

1. Five fallen—Egypt, Assyria, Babylon, Medo-Persia, and Greece
2. Sixth reigns—Rome
3. Seventh yet to come—with a brief reign. This seventh will be taken over by the eighth.
4. Eighth—Scarlet Beast; the Antichrist who will rule over ten kings (Daniel 2:24–45; "ten toes") and will war against the Lamb. The Antichrist will use world religion for his purposes and then discard her and demand that he alone be worshiped at the midpoint of the tribulation. He will become a global leader.

Revelation 18—Commercial Babylon

Commercial Babylon, a "great city," falls in one day at the end of the tribulation. Is this a literal city or just symbolic? It definitely represents economic collapse. Babylon, in all its various aspects, stands for what Jesus Christ called the "world." The merchants of the world mourn; no one is left to buy their goods. God judges her for the sake of His people.

The fate of Babylon: Much of Revelation is written in symbolic terms. At one point, the city of Babylon played a huge role in OT prophecy, but the question is, will the physical city of Babylon actually play a role in end-time prophecy, or is the name *Babylon* simply used in Revelation to refer to evil and all those in opposition to God? Theologians differ in their opinions.

Isaiah prophesied the fate of Babylon:

Behold, I will stir up the Medes against them, which shall not regard silver; and as for gold, they shall not delight in it. Their bows also shall dash the young men to pieces; and they shall have no pity on the fruit of the womb; their eyes shall not spare children.

And Babylon, the glory of kingdoms, the beauty of the Chaldees' excellency, *shall be as when God overthrew Sodom and Gomorrah. It shall never be inhabited,* neither shall it be dwelt in from generation to generation: neither shall the Arabian pitch tent there; neither shall the shepherds make their fold there. But wild beasts of the desert shall lie there; and their houses shall be full of doleful creatures; and owls shall dwell there, and satyrs shall dance there. And the wild beasts of the islands shall cry in their desolate houses, and dragons in their pleasant palaces: and her time is near to come, and her days shall not be prolonged. (Isaiah 13:17–22, emphasis added)

Isaiah predicted that Babylon would be destroyed so completely that it would become like Sodom and Gomorrah, and no one would ever live there again ("empty from generation to generation"), with desert animals living among the ruins. He predicted that Babylon's destruction would be so complete it would be like sweeping the land with a broom.

"I will make Babylon a desolate place of owls, filled with swamps and marshes. I will sweep the land with the broom of destruction. I, the Lord of Heaven's Armies, have spoken!" (Isaiah 14:23 NLT)

Jeremiah prophesied several times about the fate of Babylon. "And it shall come to pass, when seventy years are accomplished, that I will punish the king of Babylon, and that nation, saith the Lord, for their iniquity, and the land of the Chaldeans, and will make it perpetual desolations" (Jeremiah 25:12).

Similar to Isaiah, Jeremiah prophesied the destruction of Babylon would be so great and permanent "that no one would ever live there again."

The word that the Lord spake against Babylon and against the land of the Chaldeans by Jeremiah the prophet. Declare ye among the nations, and publish, and set up a standard; publish, and conceal not: say, Babylon is taken, Bel is confounded, Merodach is broken in pieces; her idols are confounded, her images are broken in pieces. For out of the north there cometh up a nation against her, which shall make her land desolate, and none shall dwell therein: they shall remove, they shall depart, both man and beast. (Jeremiah 50:1–3)

When Jeremiah said, "Babylon is taken," he meant it would fall. He went on to say how their false gods, Bel and Merodach, would be disgraced and destroyed. He too says the land will be "desolate."

Later in the same chapter, Jeremiah prophesied like Isaiah:

Therefore the wild beasts of the desert with the wild beasts of the islands shall dwell there, and the owls shall dwell therein: and it shall be no more inhabited for ever; neither shall it be dwelt in from generation to generation. As God overthrew Sodom and Gomorrah and the neighbour cities thereof, saith the Lord; so shall no man abide there, neither shall any son of man dwell therein. (Jeremiah 50:39–40)

The implication is that the destruction of Babylon would be so complete that it would lie desolate forever. In the next chapter, Jeremiah went on to say about Babylon, "'When I am finished, you will be nothing but a heap of burnt rubble. You will be desolate forever. Even your stones will never again be used for building. You will be completely wiped out,' says the Lord" (Jeremiah 51:25–26 NLT).

At the end of the chapter, we find out that God told Jeremiah to write down the prophecies against Babylon on a scroll, which Jeremiah gave to Seriah, an official who went to Babylon with Zedekiah. He told Seriah the following: "When you get to Babylon, read aloud everything on this scroll. Then say, 'Lord, you have said that you will destroy Babylon so that neither people nor animals will remain here. She will lie empty and abandoned forever.' When you have finished reading the scroll, tie it to a stone and throw it into the Euphrates River. Then say, 'In this same way Babylon and her people will sink, never again to rise, because of the disasters I will bring upon her'" (Jeremiah 51:61–64 NLT).

The word *forever* recurs repeatedly in these prophecies. Does this mean forever in the sense of the empire of Babylon in the lifetimes of those spoken to, or did it mean forever, as until the end of time? Historically, we know that the Babylonian army destroyed the Assyrian Empire between 612 BC and 605 BC, and Babylon became the capital of the Neo-Babylonian Empire until 539 BC. Babylon was known for its famous Hanging Gardens, one of the Seven Wonders of the Ancient World. In 539 BC, Cyrus the Great, king of Persia, conquered the Neo-Babylonian Empire. The walls of the city of Babylon were thought to be impenetrable, but Cyrus designed an ingenious plan. He diverted the Euphrates River upstream. Then, during a national feast, his army entered the city by way of the riverbed and conquered the outskirts of the city while the celebrating continued in the city center!

All that remains of the ancient city is broken mud-brick buildings and debris. They are located in Hillah, Iraq, some fifty-three miles south of Bagdad. Although the ancient city was divided in two parts on the east and west sides of the Euphrates, over time the river has shifted, leaving most of the west side of the old city under water. Very little of the city has been excavated. The prophecies of Isaiah and Jeremiah were fulfilled exactly.

So I return to my question: What does *forever* mean? What has been happening in the area of ancient Babylon? In 1978, Saddam Hussein's government began the Archaeological Restoration of Babylon Project. This resulted in the construction of the Southern Palace of Nebuchandnezzar, the Processional Way, the Lion of Babylon, and an amphitheater. He intended to also reconstruct the Hanging Gardens, as well as a large ziggurat, but this never happened. No further building has taken place. In 2009 the site was opened for tourists. Will ancient Babylon rise again?

New York Times best-selling author Joel C. Rosenberg, in his book *The Last Jihad* (2002), portrayed the destruction of Babylon by the Medo-Persian army as a prefigurement of an end-time destruction. In this fictional book, the city of Babylon is rebuilt. Pointing out that in 2002, President George W. Bush named Iraq, Iran, and North Korea as the "Axis of Evil," Rosenberg hypothesizes that the US president will, at some point, be forced to launch nuclear missiles at Iraq, bringing about the completion of Isaiah's and Jeremiah's prophecies regarding Babylon. He takes the prophecies in

Revelation 18 and 19 literally and believes they refer to the actual city of Babylon, which will have been rebuilt. Perhaps. Only time will tell.

Revelation 19—Victory in heaven

A vast crowd in heaven is seen praising God—"Alleluia: for the Lord God omnipotent reigneth."

The wedding feast of the Lamb—the marriage of the church, His bride, to Jesus. In the Old Testament, Israel is presented as God's wife, who is often unfaithful (Hosea 2:19–20; Isaiah 54:5; Ezekiel 16). In the New Testament, the church is presented as the fiancée of Jesus, awaiting this day of marriage (2 Corinthians 11:2; Ephesians 5:25–32). Our groom will come for us and take us to the marriage feast, which lasts throughout all eternity.

Zechariah 12 speaks of Israel's return to God and their acceptance of Jesus as the Messiah. He prophesied that the day would come when Israel will mourn the one they "pierced." Then, in Zechariah 13 we read how God will cleanse them:

> In that day there shall be a fountain opened to the house of David and to the inhabitants of Jerusalem for sin and for uncleanness. And it shall come to pass in that day, saith the Lord of hosts, that I will cut off the names of the idols out of the land, and they shall no more be remembered: and also I will cause the prophets and the unclean spirit to pass out of the land. (Zechariah 13:1–2)

All the people will be cleansed of not only their sins but also their impurities. God is going to erase idol worship from the land completely, to such an extent that the people will not even remember the names of the idols. In OT times, false prophets were often a big problem and led the people astray. Well, they will be gone too.

The church has to be made ready, sanctified, and cleansed with the washing of water by the Word—holy and without blemish. She wears "fine linen," which refers to the righteous acts of the saints, which were prepared for us to do before the foundation of the world (Ephesians 2:10).

Isaiah described this banquet:

> And in this mountain shall the Lord of hosts make unto all people a feast of fat things, a feast of wines on the lees, of fat things full of marrow, of wines on the lees well refined. And he will destroy in this mountain the face of the covering cast over all people, and the vail that is spread over all nations. He will swallow up death in victory; and the Lord God will wipe away tears from off all faces; and the rebuke of his people shall he take away from off all the earth: for the Lord hath spoken it. (Isaiah 25:6–8)

This banquet is going to be in Jerusalem. God is going to serve the best foods and well-aged "wines on the lees." The gloom and shadow of death currently hanging over the earth will be gone; death will be gone. There will be no more tears.

For a period of time, my wife and I were part owners of an Italian restaurant. I functioned as the wine buyer and became thoroughly immersed in Italian wines. Wine became one of my passions. Since my background was in biochemistry, I became fascinated by how wines are made. When I first read this passage in Isaiah, and it spoke of well-aged "wines on the lees," I wasn't exactly sure what that meant, so I visited a local winery that a friend of mine owns. I found out that the lees, or dregs, are made up of dead yeast and particulate matter that remain in the wine after completing the fermentation process. Once the wine is placed in barrels, the dead yeast and any particulate matter settle out over time as the lees or dregs. The wine is allowed to remain in contact with the lees for a time, which increases the wine's complexity and substance. Hence, Jesus in not just serving any wine at this banquet but specially aged wine of incredible complexity. I wonder sometimes if He might just have had a few bottles of the wine He made at the wedding of Cana. Imagine the opportunity to taste a wine over two thousand years old!

Who wouldn't want to attend a great banquet? Solomon represented God metaphorically as "Lady Wisdom," a woman of great hospitality in Proverbs.

Lady Wisdom has built and furnished her home; it's supported by seven hewn timbers. The banquet meal is ready to be served: lamb roasted, wine poured out, table set with silver and flowers. Having dismissed her serving maids, Lady Wisdom goes to town, stands in a prominent place, and invites everyone within sound of her voice:

"Are you confused about life, don't know what's going on? Come with me, oh come, have dinner with me! I've prepared a wonderful spread—fresh-baked bread, roast lamb, carefully selected wines. Leave your impoverished confusion and live! Walk up the street to a life with meaning." (Proverbs 9:1–6 MSG)

What an incredible invitation! This is an invitation not just to a great banquet but to a great life in the kingdom of God. God invites "everyone." And He has "carefully selected wines" in addition to the very best food.

I believe Jesus had Proverbs 9 in mind when he told the parable of the great feast in Luke 14:

And when one of them that sat at meat with him heard these things, he said unto him, "Blessed is he that shall eat bread in the kingdom of God." Then said he unto him, "A certain man made a great supper, and bade many: And sent his servant at supper time to say to them that were bidden, 'Come; for all things are now ready.' And they all with one consent began to make excuse. The first said unto him, 'I have bought a piece of ground, and I must needs go and see it: I pray thee have me excused.' And another said, 'I have bought five yoke of oxen, and I go to prove them: I pray thee have me excused.' And another said, 'I have married a wife, and therefore I cannot come.' So that servant came, and shewed his lord these things. Then the master of the house being angry said to his servant, 'Go out quickly into the streets and lanes of the city, and bring in hither the poor, and the maimed, and the halt, and the blind.' And the servant said, 'Lord, it is done as thou hast commanded, and yet there is room.' And the lord said unto the servant, 'Go out into the highways and hedges, and compel them to come in, that my house may be filled. For I say unto you, That none of those men which were bidden shall taste of my supper.'" (Luke 14:15–24)

The invitation is to everyone. The excuses that each of these three men made were weak at best. How sad the distractions of this world have such a pull on so many. Once this banquet is served, and they realize they will miss out, imagine the grief and great sadness. The apostle Paul said that as believers our citizenship is in heaven and that we live as aliens on earth now. We need to get our priorities in order now. To be prepared for what's coming, we need to turn our hearts completely to God. We need to build our houses, so to speak, upon the Rock (Jesus Christ) and put our faith completely in Him. If we do this, He promises to be with us, even through the valley of the shadow of death (Psalm 23). Whether we survive or have the privilege of being martyred for our faith, as Paul said, death holds no sting for us. For us, death is but a door that takes us from this temporal existence to our eternal existence.

During the tribulation, as the world becomes progressively more evil, it will become more and more politically incorrect to be a Christian. Christian views will fly in the face of the "new morality." Christians actually may be seen as enemies of the state. This will lead to greater persecution of the church. Will believers be ready?

I believe two crises currently face the church in the USA. One is what I call the crisis of infancy, and the other is the crisis of mediocrity. They are related and interconnected. Many people have come into our churches and have found God, which is terrific. Once saved, however, many become complacent and grow very little. This is not a new problem. The apostle Paul encountered it in some of his church plants. He spoke to one of his churches and essentially told the people the following: "You people are still drinking baby's milk. By now you should be eating meat!" He was speaking of their spiritual immaturity. I see this all the time. Many believers have been in church for years, perhaps their entire lives, but they have failed to grow up spiritually. This phenomenon leads to the crisis of mediocrity.

When was the last time you went into a coffee shop and said, "I don't want a hot cup of coffee, and I don't want iced coffee. I want lukewarm coffee"? Nobody does that! In fact, Jesus spoke to the church at Laodicea and said, "I know thy works, that thou art neither cold nor hot: I would thou wert cold or hot. So then because thou art lukewarm, and neither cold nor hot, I will spue thee out of my mouth" (Revelation 3:15–16). That was Jesus's condemnation of mediocrity. How will immature, mediocre believers ever be able to stand strong for God, demonstrating their faith in the face of persecution? The answer is, they won't. In fact, Paul predicted what has been called the *great apostasy*. "For that day shall not come, except there come a falling away first" (2 Thessalonians 2:3). What Paul is saying is that a time is coming when many will fall away and desert God.

Dietrich Bonhoeffer was a German pastor and theologian who opposed the Nazis during World War II. He is best known for his book *The Cost of Discipleship*. He was arrested in April 1943 by the Gestapo and executed by hanging on April 9, 1945. I remember watching a movie about his life. On the day of his execution, as he and a Gestapo official looked at the gallows, the official said, "This is it, Dietrich; this is the end." Bonhoeffer smiled and responded, "No, this is just the beginning!" After making that statement, he walked resolutely to the gallows and was hanged. The ability to stare death confidently in the face is a powerful witness to non-Christians. I believe we have lost something that the early church possessed. Maybe it's because those early Christians faced persecution in a way we haven't in the USA. They saw their day of martyrdom, if it came, as their day of victory. I have never heard that sermon preached.

God will use this time of persecution to refine and purify His bride, the church. Those who persist and "overcome"—the church—will be a powerful, respected force on earth. People may not like believers and even may persecute them, but they will respect them.

Jesus Christ's Second Coming

We saw in Revelation 14 how Jesus came as the righteous judge, and I shared some of the Old Testament prophecies that predicted and described His Second Coming. Now we are given more details. A number of events will occur at Jesus's Second Coming, and it is impossible to put them all in exact order. Nevertheless, we have been given several pictures of what will transpire.

The apostle Paul told believers in Corinth,

> Behold, I shew you a mystery; We shall not all sleep, but we shall all be changed, In a moment, in the twinkling of an eye, at the last trump: for the trumpet shall sound, and the dead shall be raised incorruptible, and we shall be changed. For this corruptible must put on incorruption, and this mortal must put on immortality. So when this corruptible shall have put on incorruption, and this mortal shall have put on immortality, then shall be brought to pass the saying that is written, Death is swallowed up in victory. (1 Corinthians 15:51–54)

Similarly, Paul told the church at Thessalonica,

> For this we say unto you by the word of the Lord, that we which are alive and remain unto the coming of the Lord shall not prevent them which are asleep. For the Lord himself shall descend from heaven with a shout, with the voice of the archangel, and with the trump of God: and the dead in Christ shall rise first: Then we which are alive and remain shall be caught up together with them in the clouds, to meet the Lord in the air: and so shall we ever be with the Lord. (1 Thessalonians 4:15–17)

Paul made it clear that first those believers who died will be raised from the dead first, and then those believers alive on earth when Jesus returns will be caught up with Him. They will all be transformed into immortal bodies that will never die. It will happen very fast—"in the twinkling of an eye."

Jesus returns to a hostile earth in power and glory. He comes first to the Mount of Olives. Zechariah described how the Mount of Olives will split apart, forming an east-to-west valley as half the mountain moves north and the other half moves south. All the nations will gather and fight in Jerusalem. Many will die or be taken captive, and others will flee through the valley created by the split. Then "the Lord my God shall come, and all the saints with thee" (Zechariah 14:1–5).

Daniel predicted this time as well:

> And at that time shall Michael stand up, the great prince which standeth for the children of thy people: and there shall be a time of trouble, such as never was since there was a nation even to that same time: and at that time thy people shall be delivered, every one that shall be found written in the book. And many of them that sleep in the dust of the earth shall awake, some to everlasting life, and some to shame and everlasting contempt. And they that be wise shall shine as the brightness of the firmament; and they that turn many to righteousness as the stars for ever and ever. (Daniel 12:1–3)

Daniel also called it "the shattering of the holy people" (Daniel 12:7 NLT), which will last three and a half years. He comes *to make His name known to His adversaries,* and all the nations tremble, just as Isaiah predicted. "Oh that thou wouldest rend [burst from] the heavens, that thou wouldest come down, that the mountains might flow down at thy presence, As when the melting fire burneth, the fire causeth the waters to boil, to make thy name known to thine adversaries, that the nations may tremble at thy presence!" (Isaiah 64:1–2).

After being hard-pressed by the Antichrist, *the Jews will finally say, "Blessed is He who comes in the name of the Lord!"*—just like Jesus predicted and as was recorded by Matthew (Matthew 23:39). Isaiah also looked forward to this day: "Powerful kings and mighty nations will satisfy your every need, as though you were a child nursing at the breast of a queen. You will know at last that I, the Lord, am your Savior and your Redeemer, the Mighty One of Israel" (Isaiah 60:16 NLT).

Zechariah prophesied, "And I will pour upon the house of David, and upon the inhabitants of Jerusalem, the spirit of grace and of supplications: and they shall look upon me whom they have pierced, and they shall mourn for him, as one mourneth for his only son, and shall be in bitterness for him, as one that is in bitterness for his firstborn" (Zechariah 12:10).

The day is coming when the Jews will recognize their Messiah, whom they rejected. When they realize who Jesus really is, there will be great mourning throughout the land. Heaven is opened, and Jesus comes with the armies of heaven, riding a white horse and wearing crowns and a robe dipped in blood. His name is "Faithful and True," and His title is "the Word of God." He comes demanding attention and submission and to judge a rebellious world. "And out of his mouth goeth a sharp sword, that with it he should smite the nations: and he shall rule them with a rod of iron: and he treadeth the winepress of the fierceness and wrath of Almighty God" (Revelation 19:15). Notice that Jesus never draws a sword. He only needs to speak as He did in creation.

He will rule with a rod of iron as King of Kings (Psalm 2). The day of God's patience has ended.

Ezekiel was given a vision of Jesus's Second Coming: "Suddenly, the glory of the God of Israel appeared from the east. The sound of his coming was like the roar of rushing waters, and the whole landscape shone with his glory. This vision was just like the others I had seen, first by the Kebar River and then when he came to destroy Jerusalem. I fell face down on the ground. And the glory of the Lord came into the Temple through the east gateway" (Ezekiel 43:2–4 NLT).

After landing on the Mount of Olives, Jesus will cross the Kidron Valley and enter the Old City of Jerusalem through the Eastern Gate (Golden Gate), as He did on Palm Sunday prior to His Crucifixion. Then He will enter the third (Ezekiel's) temple, and "the glory of the Lord" will fill it.

Zechariah prophesied regarding Jesus's first coming and Second Coming: "Rejoice greatly, O daughter of Zion; shout, O daughter of Jerusalem: behold, thy King cometh unto thee: he is just, and having salvation; lowly, and riding upon an ass, and upon a colt the foal of an ass" (Zechariah 9:9).

First, Jesus came as the righteous, humble suffering servant, and now he returns as the victorious King of Kings. The third temple becomes the millennial temple that Jesus will enter, bringing God's glory into it. When Jesus returns, no one will be able to deny the truth of who He is.

Look, a righteous king is coming! And honest princes will rule under him. Each one will be like a shelter from the wind and a refuge from the storm, like streams of water in the desert and the shadow of a great rock in a parched land. Then everyone who has eyes will be able to see the truth, and everyone who has ears will be able to hear it. Even the hotheads will be full of sense and understanding. Those who stammer will speak out plainly. (Isaiah 32:1–4 NLT)

In view of all the corrupt governments throughout the history of the world, having honest princes rule on the earth under the watchful eye of the righteous King will be a breath of fresh air.

War—the Beast and the false prophet are captured and cast alive into the lake of fire. The rest of their armies are killed by the sword in Jesus's mouth. There really is *no* battle!

Revelation 20—Christ's millennial reign

Satan is bound for one thousand years and thrown into the "bottomless pit," where he will not be able to deceive anyone throughout the millennium. Luke reported in his Gospel an event in which Jesus cast out many demons from a man in the region of the Gadarenes, which was located on the southeast side of the Sea of Galilee (Luke 8:26–37). The demons called themselves *Legion* because there were so many of them. When they begged Jesus not to send them into the bottomless pit, Jesus permitted them to enter a herd of pigs. Then they ran over the cliff and drowned in the lake.

This is not punishment but restraint. Satan had tried to appear as God's opposite, but he never was. Satan also had tried to imprison Jesus in a tomb, but he could not. Satan will join other angels that have been bound, as described by Jude: "And the angels which kept not their first estate, but left their own habitation, he hath reserved in everlasting chains under darkness unto the judgment of the great day" (Jude 1:6). This verse speaks of angels who left the domain where they belonged and whom God imprisoned. They await judgment day.

First resurrection—This is the resurrection of all believers who have died throughout history, who will reign with Jesus Christ for one thousand years. Jesus said, "Marvel not at this: for the hour is coming, in the which all that are in the graves shall hear his voice, And shall come forth; they that have done good, unto the resurrection of life; and they that have done evil, unto the resurrection of damnation" (John 5:28–29).

Similarly, the apostle Paul prophesied,

> And now, dear brothers and sisters, we want you to know
> what will happen to the believers who have died so you
> will not grieve like people who have no hope. For since we
> believe that Jesus died and was raised to life again, we also
> believe that when Jesus returns, God will bring back with
> him the believers who have died. We tell you this directly
> from the Lord: We who are still living when the Lord
> returns will not meet him ahead of those who have died.
> For the Lord himself will come down from heaven with a
> commanding shout, with the voice of the archangel, and
> with the trumpet call of God. *First, the believers who have
> died will rise from their graves. Then, together with them, we
> who are still alive and remain on the earth will be caught up in
> the clouds to meet the Lord in the air.* Then we will be with the
> Lord forever. So encourage each other with these words. (1
> Thessalonians 4:13–18 NLT, emphasis added)

Many Christians believe in what is called the *rapture*. The word comes
from the Vulgate translation of the Bible; in 1 Thessalonians 4:17, the Greek
word *harpazo* is translated as *rapturo*, literally meaning "to snatch out or
away." Many English translations render this word as "caught up." The Bible
clearly teaches that believers will be caught up by Christ when He returns.
The key question is, when will this occur? Those who embrace the term
rapture usually place the time of its occurrence just prior to the seven-year
tribulation period, and hence, it is called the pretribulation rapture. For this
to be true, Jesus has to come twice.

Those who believe in the pretribulation rapture believe that when
Jesus comes the first time, He does not come all the way down to earth,
but believers are caught up to Him in the sky and taken to heaven. They
emphasize that Jesus's purpose in doing this is to rescue believers from the
midst of all the judgments coming on the earth during the tribulation. The
passages used to support this are found in 1 Thessalonians 5:1–11, especially
verses 9–11:

"For God hath not appointed us to wrath, but to obtain salvation by our Lord Jesus Christ, Who died for us, that, whether we wake or sleep, we should live together with him. Wherefore comfort yourselves together, and edify one another, even as also ye do."

In other words, because of what Jesus did for us, God will not pour our His wrath (anger) upon us. Rather, when Jesus returns, we will live with Him forever. This fact should provide incredible comfort to all believers. Although unbelievers will be shocked by His coming, believers will not be, for they will have recognized the signs He predicted. Unbelievers will be saying, "Peace and safety," but then destruction will come suddenly, like the sudden onset of the labor pains of a pregnant woman. The only support for a possible pretribulation rapture that I see is that His coming occurs during a time when things seem quiet and peaceful. Jesus spoke of these "birth pains" in Matthew 24:8. However, Jesus went on to say in verse 9, "But all this is only the first of the birth pains, with more to come. Then you will be arrested, persecuted, and killed. You will be hated all over the world because you are my followers" (NLT). This does not sound much like being protected from persecution.

Another verse used to support the pretribulation rapture concept is in Luke 21:36, where we read, "Watch ye therefore, and pray always, that ye may be accounted worthy to escape all these things that shall come to pass, and to stand before the Son of man."

Again, I am not sure this is promising us protection from persecution, but we are promised protection from the judgments that fall on the earth during the tribulation. The Bible states the saints will be sealed and thereby protected from judgment but not necessarily from persecution. There is a difference.

In Revelation 6:9, we saw "the souls of them that were slain for the word of God" (i.e., martyred) under the altar in heaven. They cry out to God, asking for His judgment on those who persecuted them. In Revelation 6:11, God answers by saying this: "And white robes were given unto every one of them; and it was said unto them, that they should rest yet for a little season, until their fellow servants also and their brethren, that should be killed as they were, should be fulfilled."

God says to the martyrs, "Just wait for a little while. Your number is not yet complete. There are more martyrs coming." This does not sound like being caught up and taken out of trouble.

Although I would love to believe that Jesus comes twice—once to rapture us and then His Second Coming—I don't believe the Bible supports this for a number of reasons. While the apostle Paul was in prison, he wrote to Timothy, "Yea, and all that will live godly in Christ Jesus shall suffer persecution" (2 Timothy 3:12). I mentioned the crisis of infancy; that is, many people get saved but never really grow up in the Lord to become mature Christians. They remain baby Christians. Many do not want to hear about persecution, let alone experience it. However, the Bible literally promises us persecution if we truly follow Christ. In the Sermon on the Mount, Jesus taught, "Blessed are those who are persecuted for righteousness' sake; for theirs is the kingdom of heaven" (Matthew 5:10). Jesus made it quite clear to His followers that they would be criticized, denounced, denigrated, abused, and maybe even killed, but there would be tremendous blessing, in that they would receive the kingdom of heaven.

Life is always a matter of choice between the things of the earth and the things of God. Who will you serve—the devil or God? This is pointed out quite clearly in Revelation.

> And all the people who belong to this world worshiped the beast. They are the ones whose names were not written in the Book of Life that belongs to the Lamb who was slaughtered before the world was made. Anyone with ears to hear should listen and understand. Anyone who is destined for prison will be taken to prison. Anyone destined to die by the sword will die by the sword. This means that God's holy people must endure persecution patiently and remain faithful. (Revelation 13:8–10 NLT)

Also, in chapter 14 we read, "This means that God's holy people must endure persecution patiently, obeying his commands and maintaining their faith in Jesus" (Revelation 14:12 NLT).

In ancient times, sickness and calamities were often seen and interpreted to mean God's disfavor. The apostle Paul was criticized by the believers in the church at Corinth because they saw that he was being persecuted, and they thought this represented God's disfavor. However, Paul pointed out, "Therefore I take pleasure in infirmities, in reproaches, in necessities, in persecutions, in distresses for Christ's sake: for when I am weak, then am I strong" (2 Corinthians 12:10).

Even today, we sometimes equate wealth and material success with the blessing of God. This may be true, but as Paul pointed out, this is not always the case. Rather, he focused on God's power at work in his life and the ability to endure persecution through strength provided by the Holy Spirit.

Matthew 10:22 states, "And ye shall be hated of all men for my name's sake: but he that endureth to the end shall be saved."

Revelation 2:10 states, "Fear none of those things which thou shalt suffer: behold, the devil shall cast some of you into prison, that ye may be tried; and ye shall have tribulation ten days: be thou faithful unto death, and I will give thee a crown of life."

Paul wrote to the church in Philippi, "For unto you it is given in the behalf of Christ, not only to believe on him, but also to suffer for his sake" (Philippians 1:29).

These verses—and many more—make it clear that if we choose to follow Christ by living a godly life, then we can expect to be persecuted. During the period of the tribulation, believers either will be sealed with the "seal of the living God" (Revelation 7:2–3), which will protect them from God's judgments coming on the earth, or with the mark of the Beast (Revelation 13:16–17; 14:9–10). There may be no middle ground. It is unclear whether there might be unbelievers who choose not to take the mark of the Beast. Just as God seals His own, so Satan will create a counterfeit seal to seal his own.

Paul wrote to the believers in Thessalonica, "How you are looking forward to the coming of God's Son from heaven—Jesus, whom God raised from the dead. He is the one who has rescued us from the terrors of the coming judgment" (1 Thessalonians 1:10 NLT).

Some theologians have used this to support a rapture, but we must be clear about what Paul said. He was speaking of the judgments that would come on earth, not about persecution. Again, there is a big difference. Similarly, they use the following verse to support the same thing: "Because you have obeyed my command to persevere, I will protect you from the great time of testing that will come upon the whole world to test those who belong to this world" (Revelation 3:10 NLT).

But note that the "time of testing" (judgment) will come upon the whole world—that is, "those who belong to this world"—a world that takes the mark of the Beast, not on those sealed by God.

Some theologians state that because the word *church* or *churches* does not appear in Revelation from chapter 4 on that the description of the tribulation in the next eighteen chapters means the church is gone and has been taken out or raptured. They believe that those martyred for Christ during the tribulation period are those who become believers during the tribulation.

In the finally analysis, I would love to believe in the rapture of the church, but I believe it is inconsistent with what scripture teaches overall. I hope I am incorrect. My main concern is that those Christians who embrace the rapture, if it does not occur, will not be prepared for the persecution to come.

The East Gate will be closed forever. Ezekiel predicted the following:

> Then he brought me back the way of the gate of the outward sanctuary which looketh toward the east; and it was shut. Then said the Lord unto me; This gate shall be shut, it shall not be opened, and no man shall enter in by it; because the Lord, the God of Israel, hath entered in by it, therefore it shall be shut. (Ezekiel 44:1–2)

The current Eastern Gate (Golden Gate or Beautiful Gate) was built in the sixth or seventh century AD and faces east across the Kidron Valley toward the Mount of Olives. It is the oldest of the eight gates in the Old City wall and the only one that is completely sealed shut. Suleiman the Magnificent, a sultan of the Ottoman Empire, sealed it in AD 1540–1541. It is believed he sealed it to prevent the fulfillment of Jewish tradition, which says the Messiah will pass through it when He enters Jerusalem.

All four Gospel writers record when Jesus rode into Jerusalem through the Eastern Gate on Palm Sunday (Matthew 21; Mark 11; Luke 19; John 12). That gate was built by Solomon and probably repaired by Nehemiah. It is located underground, below the present gate. The apostle John recorded that the day prior to Jesus's entry into Jerusalem, He was staying in Bethany at the home of Lazarus, whom He had raised from the dead. We read, "Then took Mary a pound of ointment of spikenard, very costly, and anointed the feet of Jesus, and wiped his feet with her hair: and the house was filled with the odour of the ointment" (John 12:3).

Nard was a very expensive ointment imported from India. It is estimated that the twelve-ounce jar was worth a year's wages! The Hebrew term *Messiah* (in Greek, *Christos*) literally means "the anointed one." To be anointed was to be dedicated to God, and that person was either a king or priest. In the case of Jesus, He is both our high priest and our King. When Jesus rode into Jerusalem, the smell of the nard would have been evident to the people near Him, and they would have identified it as a sign of His Kingship.

Daniel predicted that Jesus, "'the Anointed One,' will be killed, appearing to have accomplished nothing" (Daniel 9:25–26 NLT). Jesus did come, He was killed, and even His disciples were temporarily dismayed after His Crucifixion. However, the resurrection changed everything.

Ezekiel predicted the dimensions of Jerusalem: "The distance around the entire city will be 6 miles. And from that day the name of the city will be 'The Lord Is There'" (Ezekiel 48:35 NLT).

Death and the grave are thrown into the lake of fire.

God will draw the remaining scattered Jews a second time to Israel from Assyria, Egypt, Ethiopia, Elam (Iran), Babylonia, Hamath, and distant coastlands (Isaiah 11:11).

> And it shall come to pass, when ye be multiplied and increased in the land, in those days, saith the Lord, they shall say no more, "The ark of the covenant of the Lord:" neither shall it come to mind: neither shall they remember it; neither shall they visit it; neither shall that be done any more. At that time they shall call Jerusalem the throne of the Lord; and all the nations shall be gathered unto it, to the name of the Lord, to Jerusalem: neither shall they walk any more after the imagination of their evil heart. (Jeremiah 3:16–17)

The ark of the covenant was a gold-plated acacia-wood chest described in the book of Exodus. It contained the two stone tablets of the Ten Commandments brought down from Mount Sinai by Moses, Aaron's rod, and a vessel of manna. Great power was present with the ark since God's presence rested upon the mercy seat, which was the golden lid with two golden cherubim. When the Israelites wandered in the Sinai Desert for forty years, the ark was carried twenty-six hundred feet in front of the people and went with the army into battle. It was first located in the tabernacle. When Solomon dedicated the temple, the ark was placed in a special room called the Holy of Holies. Scripture records that after the ark was placed there by the priests, "the house was filled with a cloud, even the house of the Lord; So that the priests could not stand to minister by reason of the cloud: for the glory of the Lord had filled the house of God" (2 Chronicles 5:13–14 NLT).

Under the reign of a series of evil kings, the ark must have been taken from the temple because 2 Chronicles 35:3 states that King Josiah commanded that the ark be brought back into the temple. Following the destruction of Jerusalem and the temple by the Babylonians in 587 BC, there is no further mention of the ark. Many theories have developed regarding its whereabouts, if it even still exists. Some rabbis believe that it was taken to Babylon along with the temple treasures, but I tend to agree with the rabbis who believe Josiah hid the ark somewhere deep in the Temple Mount to prevent it from being taken.

A fascinating read on this subject is Joel Rosenberg's book *The Copper Scroll*, published in 2006. In addition to the Dead Sea Scrolls that were found in the caves at Qumran, another scroll of a different sort was found in 1952, called the Copper Scroll, which is currently on exhibit in the Jordan Archaeological Museum. This scroll was not written on papyrus or parchment but on copper mixed with 1 percent tin. In contrast to the other scrolls, its subject matter is quite different. It records an inventory of sixty-four locations, listing tons of silver and gold treasures. Of particular interest is the last entry, which suggests the existence of some form of duplicate scroll with more details; this scroll has never been found. Various attempts to follow the directions of the scroll in order to find the treasure have turned up nothing. In 2007, the History Channel did a series titled *Digging for the Truth*, which explored the various theories surrounding the Copper Scroll.

The potential wealth possibly hidden could be enormous, especially when one considers Solomon's wealth. It states in 1 Kings 10:23, "So king Solomon exceeded all the kings of the earth for riches and for wisdom." Solomon's kingdom would have been the wonder of the ancient world at the time, attracting international attention. When the queen of Sheba visited Solomon, she brought him considerable gold and precious jewels. Subsequently, much of this treasure was captured by invaders or bartered by Israel's kings for protection. However, even under Roman rule during the time of Jesus, the Jews contributed significant wealth to the temple treasury yearly when they paid the temple tax. Although much of this wealth was carried off to Rome when Jerusalem and the temple were destroyed in AD 70, it is possible some was also hidden beneath the Temple Mount.

The present Temple Mount in Jerusalem contains many subterranean chambers that are filled with rock and debris. Could one of them hold the ark and some of the temple treasures that were stored there to prevent foreign invaders from taking them? Perhaps. Currently, many of these underground passageways are off limits to exploration, due to Muslim control of the Temple Mount. As the Orthodox Jews make preparations to build the third temple, the discovery of the ark would be of great significance. In the New Jerusalem, however, as Jeremiah prophesied, "you will no longer wish for 'the good old days' when you possessed the Ark of the Lord's Covenant. You will not miss those days or even remember them, and there will be no need to rebuild the Ark" (Jeremiah 3:16–17 NLT).

Celebration of the Festival of Shelters—Zechariah stated that during the millennium, even the survivors of the enemies that fought against Jerusalem will come to Jerusalem to worship the "King, the Lord of hosts, and to keep the feast of tabernacles" (Zechariah 14:16 NLT). The Feast of Tabernacles (Festival of Shelters) will be the only Jewish festival to be celebrated during Jesus's millennial reign. When Jesus died as the Lamb of God, He fulfilled the Passover. When we accept His sacrifice for our sins and receive salvation, the Day of Atonement is fulfilled. When He rose from the dead, he was the "first fruit" of the harvest of souls fulfilling the Festival of First Harvest. And when the Holy Spirit filled the believers at Pentecost, it was fulfilled.

People will come from all over the world to Jerusalem, and out of Zion will go forth the law, and Jesus will teach His ways.

Isaiah predicted the following:

> And it shall come to pass in the last days, that the mountain of the Lord's house shall be established in the top of the mountains, and shall be exalted above the hills; and all nations shall flow unto it. And many people shall go and say, "Come ye, and let us go up to the mountain of the Lord, to the house of the God of Jacob; and he will teach

us of his ways, and we will walk in his paths: for out of Zion shall go forth the law, and the word of the Lord from Jerusalem." And he shall judge among the nations, and shall rebuke many people: and they shall beat their swords into plowshares, and their spears into pruninghooks: nation shall not lift up sword against nation, neither shall they learn war any more. (Isaiah 2:2–4; see also Micah 4:1–3)

Isaiah prophesied that Gentiles will bring wealth to Israel as gifts to God (Isaiah 60:3–16; 61:5–7).

Jesus will judge the nations and rebuke many people (Zephaniah 3:8). Conflicts will occur that He will resolve. The reign of Jesus does not change the heart of man. Citizens of the earth will still need to trust in Jesus and His work on their behalf for their personal salvation. Apparently, many will outwardly (but not inwardly) acknowledge Jesus Christ.

Jesus will bring peace to the nations, and there will be no more war. It will not be tolerated. Zechariah predicted, "I will remove the battle chariots from Israel and the warhorses from Jerusalem. I will destroy all the weapons used in battle, and your king will bring peace to the nations. His realm will stretch from sea to sea and from the Euphrates River to the ends of the earth" (Zechariah 9:10 NLT).

There will again be one language on earth. Zephaniah 3:9 states, "For then will I turn to the people a pure language, that they may all call upon the name of the Lord, to serve him with one consent."

Following the great flood, the descendants of Noah migrated eastward and settled in a land called Shinar. Genesis 11:1–9 describes how the population grew, and they all spoke the same language. One day they decided to build a great tower, or ziggurat. A ziggurat is a temple built in the form of a pyramidal tower. This was to be a symbol of their pride regarding what they could do. When God came down to see what they were up to, He realized that with one language they were capable of accomplishing anything they put their minds to. Their key problem was that they wanted to construct a tower that extended up into the "heavens." In other words, their intention was to be like God so that they did not need God.

When God saw what they were building, He gave the people multiple languages, and as a result, they scattered and settled, based upon whatever common language each group possessed. Proverbs 16:18 states, "Pride goeth before destruction, and an haughty spirit before a fall." That's exactly what happened to these people; their pride led to their downfall. The tower came to be known as the Tower of Babel because the word *Babel* means *confusion*. Zephaniah says that one day God will again give us a common language so that we can worship and serve God together.

There will be no more wild animals. The danger of predators will be gone (Isaiah 11:4–9; 65:25). Genesis 9:2–3 will be reversed, and there will be no more dread of animals. Some aspects of the curse under which we currently live will be lifted.

The earth will be full of the knowledge of the Lord.

The remnant of Israel will no longer be proud and arrogant. The prophet Zephaniah prophesied exactly the same thing:

> In that day shalt thou not be ashamed for all thy doings, wherein thou hast transgressed against me: for then I will take away out of the midst of thee them that rejoice in thy pride, and thou shalt no more be haughty because of my holy mountain. I will also leave in the midst of thee an afflicted and poor people, and they shall trust in the name of the Lord. The remnant of Israel shall not do iniquity, nor speak lies; neither shall a deceitful tongue be found in their mouth: for they shall feed and lie down, and none shall make them afraid. (Zephaniah 3:11–13)

One of Israel's biggest problems was always their pride and arrogance, which continually led to rebellion against God. A day is coming when all those who are proud and arrogant will be gone. Only the humble—those who trust in God—will remain. They will live in safety without fear.

The prophet Habakkuk prophesied the following regarding the proud: "This vision is for a future time. It describes the end, and it will be fulfilled. If it seems slow in coming, wait patiently, for it will surely take place. It will not be delayed. 'Look at the proud! They trust in themselves, and their lives are crooked. But the righteous will live by their faithfulness to God'" (Habakkuk 2:3–4 NLT).

There will be a reversal of anti-Semitism. Zechariah prophesied, "Thus saith the Lord of hosts; In those days it shall come to pass, that ten men shall take hold out of all languages of the nations, even shall take hold of the skirt of him that is a Jew, saying, We will go with you: for we have heard that God is with you" (Zechariah 8:23).

What a difference! Ten men who all speak different languages will grab onto the sleeve of one Jew because they know God is with the Jew. When times are tough, people are looking for people of faith they can hold for support. Is that the kind of relationship you have with God? Do people gravitate to you during difficult situations and ask you to pray on their behalf because they know you are connected to God?

Jesus will rule as the righteous branch and execute judgment and justice on the earth.

> Behold, the days come, saith the Lord, that I will raise unto David a righteous Branch, and a King shall reign and prosper, and shall execute judgment and justice in the earth. In his days Judah shall be saved, and Israel shall dwell safely: and this is his name whereby he shall be called, The Lord Our Righteousness. (Jeremiah 23:5–6) (See also Jeremiah 33:14–17; Isaiah 4:2; 11:1; Zechariah 3:8; 6:12; John 15:5.)

Resurrected saints will be given responsibility in the millennial kingdom, according to their faithful service (Luke 19:11–29; Revelation 20:4–6; 2:26–28; 3:12, 22; 1 Corinthians 6:2–3).

People will live much longer. "No longer will babies die when only a few days old. No longer will adults die before they have lived a full life. No longer will people be considered old at one hundred! Only the cursed will die that young!" (Isaiah 65:20 NLT).

Restoration of the land of Israel—Micah prophesied the following:

> In that day, Israel, your cities will be rebuilt, and your borders will be extended. People from many lands will come and honor you—from Assyria all the way to the towns of Egypt, from Egypt all the way to the Euphrates River, and from distant seas and mountains. But the land will

become empty and desolate because of the wickedness of those who live there. O Lord, protect your people with your shepherd's staff; lead your flock, your special possession. Though they live alone in a thicket on the heights of Mount Carmel, let them graze in the fertile pastures of Bashan and Gilead as they did long ago. "Yes," says the Lord, "I will do mighty miracles for you, like those I did when I rescued you from slavery in Egypt." All the nations of the world will stand amazed at what the Lord will do for you. They will be embarrassed at their feeble power. They will cover their mouths in silent awe, deaf to everything around them. Like snakes crawling from their holes, they will come out to meet the Lord our God. They will fear him greatly, trembling in terror at his presence. Where is another God like you, who pardons the guilt of the remnant, overlooking the sins of his special people? You will not stay angry with your people forever, because you delight in showing unfailing love. Once again you will have compassion on us. You will trample our sins under your feet and throw them into the depths of the ocean! You will show us your faithfulness and unfailing love as you promised to our ancestors Abraham and Jacob long ago. (Micah 7:11–20 NLT)

God is going to do "mighty miracles" equivalent to or maybe even greater than when He rescued the people from their captivity in Egypt. When God does this, all people from all over the world will see and recognize God's hand. It will be a literal "OMG" experience! Once again, God's unfailing love will shine and come to the rescue of His people.

His kingdom will have no end (Luke 1:32–33; 19:12–27).

There will be blessing and security for Israel (Amos 9:11–15). Israel will be the world's superpower. The center of the theocratic government will be the temple in Jerusalem. It appears that King David will have a prominent place in the millennial kingdom, ruling over Israel (Isaiah 55:3–5; Jeremiah 30:4–11; Ezekiel 34:23–31; 37:21–28; Hosea 3:5).

Post-Millennium (after the Thousand-Year Reign of Christ)

Satan is released and goes out to deceive the nations throughout the earth. It is incredible that even after Jesus has reigned perfectly on earth for one thousand years, men still rebel! Satan leads his forces and surrounds Jerusalem, wanting to destroy God's people. However, God sends fire from heaven and devours them. Again, there really is no battle. Satan is thrown into the lake of fire to be tormented day and night forever (Matthew 25:41).

Great white throne judgment—God, in all His fullness, sits on His throne (John 5:22–27). All the unbelieving dead stand before God. Books are opened, and they are judged by the things written in the books. This is no trial, only sentencing! Innocence and guilt will be evident. There will be degrees of punishment for unbelievers. These men and women lived their lives wanting to be independent of God. They wanted no part of Him. Now, God will give them exactly what they always wanted—an eternity separated from Him (Matthew 11:20–24).

Death and Hades are cast into the lake of fire—The lake of fire is referred to as Gehenna ("hell," in Greek), which referred to the Valley of Hinnom, which was outside Jerusalem's walls. It was where the pagan god Molech was worshipped, and human sacrifice occurred (2 Chronicles 28:1–3; Jeremiah 32:35). It was a garbage dump where trash burned continuously. Being cast into the lake of fire is defined as the "second death."

The judgment seat of Christ—This is only for Christians. All works will be tested by fire (i.e., all motives will be revealed), "for we shall all stand before the judgment seat of Christ" (Romans 14:10b).

"For the Son of man shall come in the glory of his Father with his angels; and then he shall reward every man according to his works" (Matthew 16:27).

"Knowing that whatsoever good thing any man doeth, the same shall he receive of the Lord, whether he be bond [slave] or free" (Ephesians 6:8).

"For we must all appear before the judgment seat of Christ; that every one may receive the things done in his body, according to that he hath done, whether it be good or bad" (2 Corinthians 5:10).

"Anyone who builds on that foundation may use a variety of materials—gold, silver, jewels, wood, hay, or straw. But on the judgment day, fire will reveal what kind of work each builder has done. The fire will show if a person's work has any value. If the work survives, that builder will receive a reward. But if the work is burned up, the builder will suffer great loss. The builder will be saved, but like someone barely escaping through a wall of flames" (1 Corinthians 3:12–15 NLT).

Revelation 21 and 22—The New Heaven and the New Earth (Eternity)

A new heaven and new earth—"And I saw a new heaven and a new earth: for the first heaven and the first earth were passed away; and there was no more sea" (Revelation 21:1).

The Old Testament prophets spoke of this new heaven and new earth as follows:

> Long ago you laid the foundation of the earth and made the heavens with your hands. They will perish, but you remain forever; they will wear out like old clothing. You will change them like a garment and discard them. But you are always the same; you will live forever. (Psalm 102:25–27 NLT)

"For, behold, I create new heavens and a new earth: and the former shall not be remembered, nor come into mind" (Isaiah 65:17; also Isaiah 66:22). Imagine how amazing the new heaven and earth will be if we don't even remember the old!

The apostle Peter had this to say: "Looking for and hasting unto the coming of the day of God, wherein the heavens being on fire shall be dissolved, and the elements shall melt with fervent heat? Nevertheless we, according to his promise, look for new heavens and a new earth, wherein dwelleth righteousness" (2 Peter 3:12–13).

What does a "new heaven" mean? The Bible refers to heaven in three ways:

1. First heaven—the earth's atmosphere (blue sky)
2. Second heaven—outer space
3. Third heaven—the place where God dwells in glory

The new heaven spoken of in Revelation refers to the first two heavens but not the third. Some theologians believe that the earth and heaven are not destroyed but completely are remade. Jesus said that heaven and earth will pass away but that His Word would never pass away (Luke 21:33). Also, when Isaiah prophesied God would create a new heaven and new earth (Isaiah 65:17), the Hebrew word he used for *create* means to "create out of nothing," not remake.

God living on the new earth—"And I heard a loud voice from the throne, saying, 'Behold, the tabernacle of God is among men, and He will dwell among them, and they shall be His people, and God Himself will be among them'" (Revelation 21:3).

The New Testament speaks about this New Jerusalem on several occasions as "the city of the living God, the heavenly Jerusalem" (Hebrews12:22), and the heavenly Jerusalem (Galatians 4:26 NLT). The apostle Paul referred to it as the place of our real citizenship (Philippians 3:20). It is a place where we will dwell in perfect community with each other and with God. It is described as being as beautiful and perfect as a bride. Just as God dwelled with the Israelites in the tabernacle, He will now dwell on earth with us. God's ultimate desire has been to dwell with His people. All that was lost due to man's sin—and with the resultant separation from God in the fall—will be regained, and our intimate relationship with God restored. Revelation 21:9–10 states that the New Jerusalem is called the bride, the Lamb's wife. Why? Because God's people will dwell there, we who are the bride of Christ.

There will be no tears, sorrow, death, pain, temple, sacrifices, sun, moon, darkness, or sin and nothing abominable.

God says, "Look, I am making everything new!" (Revelation 21:5). We appreciate this on earth in the atonement to a degree when Paul said that when we accept Christ, we become "a new creation; old things have passed away; behold all things have become new" (2 Corinthians 5:17). God will take this to a new level of experience.

God also says, "It is finished!" Jesus previously said these words on the cross.

> And he also said, "It is finished! I am the Alpha and the Omega—the Beginning and the End. To all who are thirsty I will give freely from the springs of the water of life. All who are victorious will inherit all these blessings, and I will

be their God, and they will be my children." (Revelation
21:6–7 NLT)

How many have searched for the illusive fountain of life? Well, here it is!
This fountain not only satisfies physical thirst but spiritual thirst as well. All
who have been victorious and overcome by faith trusting in Jesus may drink.

The apostle John stated, "Who is he that overcometh the world, but he
that believeth that Jesus is the Son of God?" (1 John 5:5).

The description of the New Jerusalem—Incredible brilliant light due to
God's glory; the city it is made of pure gold, like clear glass, with a street of
gold. A great high wall made of jasper, with twelve gates made of pearl (named
for each of the twelve tribes of Israel) and twelve foundation stones adorned
with precious gemstones (named for the twelve apostles—Ephesians 2:20
says the church was built upon the foundation of the apostles, with Jesus as
the cornerstone). Only the righteous are permitted to enter.

The city is 1,500 miles in length, width, and height—plenty of room for
all believers of all times.

Hebrews 11:10 states, "For he [Abraham] looked for a city which hath
foundations, whose builder and maker is God." Here it is in all its beauty and
splendor. If man has created some beautiful cities with amazing buildings,
just think what God will do. It's almost impossible to conceive of a city
of this size. The base is fifteen hundred by fifteen hundred miles square.
Fifteen hundred miles is the distance from Boston to Miami. And it is fifteen
hundred miles tall. We are not told if this is a square or pyramid; either is
possible. The new earth likely will need to be reconfigured to accommodate
this city, not to mention the atmosphere.

I remember reading about the expeditions to climb Mount Everest,
which is almost thirty thousand feet (five and a half miles). Most climbers
require supplemental oxygen to make it to the top. What will it be like in
a city that reaches fifteen hundred miles into the sky? Maybe our glorified
bodies will need less oxygen, or maybe God will also readjust the atmospheric
conditions.

There is no temple; God and the Lamb are its temple. Since the glory of
God will illuminate it, there will be no need for the sun or moon. Our focus
will be totally God—Jesus, Jesus, Jesus!

Paul explained this to the church of Ephesus:

> Now, therefore, you are no longer strangers and foreigners, but fellow citizens with the saints and members of the household of God, having been built on the foundation of the apostles and prophets, Jesus Christ Himself being the chief cornerstone, in whom the whole building, being fitted together, grows into a holy temple in the Lord, in whom you also are being built together for a dwelling place of God in the Spirit. (Ephesians 2:19–22)

We will no longer feel like foreigners and aliens, living in a country that does not suit us. Finally, we will fit perfectly in our family. It will be an experience unlike anything we could ever imagine.

Likewise, the apostle Peter wrote, "You also, as living stones, are being built up a spiritual house, a holy priesthood, to offer up spiritual sacrifices acceptable to God through Jesus Christ" (1 Peter 2:5).

We serve a living God, the one true and only God. We are described as "living stones," which make up a spiritual house, which is a priesthood that serves God. It will be our greatest joy. Heaven is often pictured with saints floating on clouds, playing harps. Nothing could be farther from the truth. When God created Adam and Eve and placed them in the garden of Eden, He came to the garden to be with them. But sin and the subsequent curse that came on the earth separated man from God. Through Jesus's death and resurrection, we have been redeemed—bought back.

On the new earth, God will live among us, not just visit us. We were designed to "live" on the earth, and that is exactly what we will do. Based upon how we lived our lives, God will assign us work to do on the new earth. The work will be significant and not associated with the toil we currently experience while under the curse. Think of all the things you enjoy doing now. I suspect you will get to do them on the new earth, plus a whole lot more.

The kings of the earth will bring their glory and honor to the New Jerusalem. Finally, all the ruling powers on earth will acknowledge Jesus, the King of all kings, and His ultimate authority.

The river of the water of life flows from the throne of God (namely, from God Himself).

> And he shewed me a pure river of water of life, clear as crystal, proceeding out of the throne of God and of the Lamb. In the midst of the street of it, and on either side of the river, was there the tree of life, which bare twelve manner of fruits, and yielded her fruit every month: and the leaves of the tree were for the healing of the nations. (Revelation 22:1–2)

A river will flow east from the throne to the Dead Sea, which will come to life and flow west to the Mediterranean Sea.

Ezekiel prophesied,

> Fishermen will stand along the shores of the Dead Sea. All the way from En-gedi to En-eglaim, the shores will be covered with nets drying in the sun. Fish of every kind will fill the Dead Sea, just as they fill the Mediterranean. But the marshes and swamps will not be purified; they will still be salty. Fruit trees of all kinds will grow along both sides of the river. The leaves of these trees will never turn brown and fall, and there will always be fruit on their branches. There will be a new crop every month, for they are watered by the river flowing from the Temple. The fruit will be for food and the leaves for healing. (Ezekiel 47:10–12)

Similarly, Zechariah prophesied, "And it shall be in that day, that living waters shall go out from Jerusalem; half of them toward the former sea [Dead Sea], and half of them toward the hinder sea [Mediterranean Sea]: in summer and in winter shall it be" (Zechariah 14:8).

Fruit trees will grow on both sides with a new crop of fruit each month. The fruit will be for food and the leaves for healing (Ezekiel 47:12).

The tree of life—Whatever God does, He always saves the very best for last. We saw this tree of life in the center of the garden of Eden (Genesis 3:22–23). Now, with sin banished, man can eat of this tree. God made time for us, yet for Him it has no relevance, since He always was, is, and always will be—the Alpha and the Omega. But apparently in the new heaven, we will still have time, as the tree of life will bear a different fruit "every month." By the act of eating, man fell into sin, but even this act will be redeemed.

I have always found it interesting that the leaves of the tree will be used for healing the nations. Could this be some form of balm that will heal past divisions among nations and the scars produced by civil wars?

There will be no more curse. We cannot even imagine what it will be like to live without being under this curse—freed from sickness, toil of inefficient work, constant friction between people, bugs tormenting us, weeds in our garden, etc.

Instead of the difficult work we face now, we will live as priests and kings, serving God with pure joy. Imagine working and being thrilled by all your activity and the result of it. And with our risen new bodies not afflicted by the effects of disease, mutations, and other maladies, we will experience a youthfulness and strength unlike anything before.

We will see God's face. This is more than just looking. It is understanding God in a way we never have before. The apostle Paul expressed this in 1 Corinthians 13:12: "For now we see through a glass, darkly; but then face to face: now I know in part; but then shall I know even as also I am known." I like how it is expressed in the New Living Translation version: "Now we see things imperfectly, like puzzling reflections in a mirror, but then we will see everything with perfect clarity. All that I know now is partial and incomplete, but then I will know everything completely, just as God now knows me completely."

I cannot imagine the intimacy we will have with God!

One day I was reflecting on my relationship with God over many years. I said to Him, "God, you are like a giant onion! I eat one layer, and then I realize there is another layer. With each layer, I come to understand you more."

He said to me, "Michael, you are right; however, you are not on the outside of the onion but on the inside in the center. After you eat one layer and grow in your understanding of Me, the next layer is even larger! This will continue throughout your life as you continue to seek me. Then, after you die, you will have all eternity to explore the depth and riches of our relationship. Unlike an onion, My layers are infinite."

Wow! That blew me away. We will live in a perfect relationship with God and fall progressively deeper and deeper in love with Him. This is our wonderful hope: "I pray that your hearts will be flooded with light so that you can understand the confident hope he has given to those he called—his holy people who are his rich and glorious inheritance" (Ephesian 1:18 NLT).

So many times we emphasize and look forward to our inheritance. But do you realize that believers are God's "rich and glorious inheritance"? Perhaps He looks forward to being with us even more than we look forward to being with Him.

His name will be written on our foreheads. Those who have been faithful throughout time will be given the privilege of wearing His name permanently. We live in the age of tattoos. People seek to express who they are individualistically, to claim some identity. We will be identified as belonging to the King—the greatest identity throughout all eternity.

There will be no night. In other words, there will be no darkness. With God's presence permeating everywhere, there will be no need for the sun or moon or any other source of light. His brilliance will be incredible. Only with our glorified bodies will we be able to exist in the presence of this brilliance. Our earthly sunglasses would be insufficient. Like the apostle Paul experienced on the road to Damascus when he saw Jesus, we too would be blinded.

We will reign with Him forever and ever. God is all about restoration. He is the God of second chances. The Bible starts in a garden of perfection and ends in paradise. As always, God doesn't just take us back but forward to something even better.

If you would like to know more about what heaven will be like, I encourage you to read *50 Days of Heaven, Reflections That Bring Eternity to Light* by Randy Alcorn (his short version) or *Heaven* (his long version).

Conclusion

In the introduction, I explained that the function of a prophet was not necessarily to predict the future but to instruct and exhort people to turn from sin and turn to God. Jeremiah did this repeatedly. Listen to his instructions:

> Thus says the Lord,
> "Stand by the ways and see and ask for the *ancient paths*,
> Where the good way is, and walk in it;
> And you will find rest for your souls."
> But they said, "We will not walk in it." (Jeremiah 6:16 NASB, emphasis added)

> For My people have forgotten Me,
> They burn incense to worthless gods
> And they have stumbled from their ways,
> From the *ancient paths*,
> To walk in bypaths,
> Not on a highway. (Jeremiah 18:15 NASB, emphasis added)

As we have seen, when God inspired His prophets to predict the future, their prophecies often involved warnings of what was to come in the hope that the people would repent and turn back to Him—that is, to get back on the "ancient paths," the tried-and-true ways of God that would provide blessings for their lives and not curses. God sent Jonah to Nineveh, the capital of Assyria, to prophesy its destruction if the people did not repent. And they did repent, at least for a time, which delayed their destruction.

When Daniel was given his vision of the tribulation period, he was told to "seal it up"—to keep it secret (Daniel 8:26). Almost seven hundred years later, however, John was instructed to do the opposite: "And he saith unto me, 'Seal not the sayings of the prophecy of this book: for the time is at hand'" (Revelation 22:10).

Jesus declared, "Behold, I am coming quickly [suddenly], and My reward is with Me, to render to every man according to what he has done. I am the Alpha and the Omega, the first and the last, the beginning and the end" (Revelation 22:12–13 NASB).

He then repeated this at the end of the chapter in verse 20. Remember—if it's repeated in scripture, it's for emphasis; it's important!

This book has given you a road map for what lies ahead. You now know what the tribulation and great tribulation are all about. You and your family can prepare. Persecution was a part of the early church and still is today in many parts of the world. Prior to Jesus's return, it will get worse. Although biblical prophecy seems complicated, especially with so many prophecies scattered throughout the Bible, I have tried to align those of the Old Testament with their New Testament counterparts. I hope you have gained an appreciation for how it all fits together. You've gained an understanding of God's strategy to restore everything and have come to recognize how this plays out in His recurrent themes of judgment, discipline, restoration, sovereignty, warning, and protection.

God wants us to live with a sense of urgency and expectancy regarding His Son's return. Whatever you need to do to get right with God—to get on the "ancient path"—do it now. Don't wait, thinking you will have time later, because when Jesus comes, it will be sudden and—for many—unexpected. It will be too late for making changes. As the book of Revelation closes, it makes it perfectly clear that you will want to be on the right side of the line.

> Blessed are those who wash their robes [keep His commandments], that they may have the right to the tree of life and may go through the gates into the city. Outside are the dogs, those who practice magic arts, the sexually immoral, the murderers, the idolaters and everyone who loves and practices falsehood. (Revelation 22:14–15 NIV)

I have been going to the same barber for over thirty-five years. I like him not just because he does a good job but also because he is fast and cheap. He cut my hair a few weeks ago, as the new year was approaching. I said, "Remember all the stir about Y2K? Everyone anticipated computer failures because the software in use represented years with two digits rather than four, and IT experts were worried that computers wouldn't be able to tell the difference between year 1900 and year 2000."

"Yes," he responded, "people feared planes would drop out of the sky!"

Fortunately, not much happened. Then I said, "Remember how people prepared for Y2K? I even bought a generator and enough food to last three months." We both thought about that for a minute or so. Then I said, "Look at all that people did to prepare for their temporal existence for Y2K, but so many people don't seem to be concerned about their eternal existence after they die. They are not preparing for it."

"What would you do?" he asked.

I explained that I had studied many of the world's religions, and I had often heard people say, "Religions are basically all alike. God is on a mountaintop, and each religion represents a different path up to God." I told him I did not believe that; the reason I am a Christian is that my God did not stay on top of the mountain but came down to me—to all of us. The Bible says that God gave His Son, Jesus, a body so He could come to earth and offer it up for us.

"What other god in the history of the world has ever done anything like that?" I asked.

He responded, "Good point. I have never heard it presented like that."

If you are a true believer in Jesus, stay on (or get back on) the ancient paths. Spend time each day reading and meditating on God's Word to nourish your spirit. Ask the Holy Spirit to show you how to "live by every word that proceeds from the mouth of the Lord" (Deuteronomy 8:3; Matthew 4:4). Live in continual fellowship with God. Live in a state of continual repentance, always turning away from sin and to God. If you have never asked the Holy Spirit to fill you completely, I encourage you to get on your knees right now and do it. I did it at age twenty-six, and my life has not been the same since!

One final invitation is given in Revelation:

> The Spirit and the bride say, "Come." Let anyone who
> hears this say, "Come." Let anyone who is thirsty come.
> Let anyone who desires drink freely from the water of life.
> (Revelations 22:17 NLT)

"Anyone" can come, if he or she "desires." Do you desire? Do you have the desire to come to Jesus and to acknowledge who He is and what He has done for you? If not, pray that the Holy Spirit will reveal Jesus to you, and put the desire deep within your heart. Get on your knees and pour your heart out to the living God, who hears and always answers your prayers.

Perhaps you have arrived at the point at which you believe that what the Bible says about Jesus is true. If so, I encourage you to pray the following prayer (or one in your own words similar to it). The exact words don't matter as much as the attitude of your heart.

Dear Jesus, I have come to realize that You and You alone are the Savior of the world. I know that God the Father sent You, His only Son, into the world to die for me and all mankind as His plan of redemption. You said that You are the way, the truth, and the life and that no one can come to the Father except by You. So I confess to You now that I am a sinner in need of Your forgiveness. I believe that Your blood offering on the cross was powerful and more than enough to cleanse me from my sin and unrighteousness. I believe that You rose from the dead and sit in heaven right now, where all authority has been given to You. And I wait with eager anticipation for Your Second Coming, Your return to earth, to set up your perfect kingdom. On that day, everyone will bow before You and confess that You are King of kings and Lord of lords.

Today, right now, I receive You as my Savior and also ask you to be Lord of my life. Please guide and direct me in every way. Fill me with Your Holy Spirit to empower me to live right. And please, Holy Spirit, instruct me day by day on how I should live so I become a true follower of Jesus Christ. Thank you, Jesus, for forgiveness. Thank you for making me into a new person who wants to serve You with all my heart. I look forward to spending eternity with You! Amen.

If you have prayed this prayer, I strongly encourage you to read the Bible every day. Remember, the words in the Bible will be *life* for you.

Several years ago I wrote a book titled *The Ancient Path: Rediscovering Manhood*. I used that book to mentor and disciple fifty men over the next eight years. I had the privilege of watching God powerfully transform many of these men into the husbands and fathers God intended them to be. The key to each man's transformation was in teaching him how to connect to God daily. To help them each do this, I developed a spiritual tool that I call Doing First Things First—Seven Minutes a Day. I held each man accountable to do this *every* day without exception. I did this because I knew I have no ability to transform anyone. That is God's job, as His Holy Spirit works within hearts. What follows is that tool. You might want to copy it or tear it out of this book and keep it in your Bible. I would encourage you to use it daily, as those fifty men did.

Doing First Things First
Seven Minutes a Day

Visualize and pray the following:

1. See Jesus standing at the door of your heart, knocking, wanting to come in (Revelation 3:20).
2. Open the door, and ask Jesus to come in. Since Jesus says that He abides in the Father and the Father abides in Him, see both of them come in.
3. Ask the Father and Jesus to sit on the throne of your heart and reign. The Holy Spirit is already there.
4. Pray:
   - Jesus, please shine Your light into all the dark corners of my heart, exposing the darkness—my sin. "Cleanse my heart, oh God, and renew a right spirit within me" (Psalm 51:10).
   - Holy Spirit, judge the thoughts and intentions of my heart. Reveal and expose them, and please transform them. Renew my mind.

- Jesus, replace my desires with Your desires, replace my passions with Your passions, and replace my will with Your will so that I can seek Your kingdom first in every way.
- Holy Spirit, fill my heart completely with Your love, and let it work so eminently within me that I will prefer You above all else and without reserve.

Open your Bible, and select a passage to read:

Pray: Holy Spirit, please give me understanding and wisdom and reveal to me the "secrets of the kingdom" (Matthew 13:11).

Think deeply and meditate on the words you have read. Recognize that the Bible is not only the written Word but the living Word of God (literally, Jesus revealed to us).

Remember this is your time with God. He loves you and wants to spend time with you. He relishes this time, and He wants to speak to you.

Sense His presence; enjoy being with Him.

Ask Him what he wants to say to you.

Listen to what He has to say.

Receive His peace that surpasses all understanding.

Only you can give God what He wants most—your personal love and affection. I'm sure God wishes we would do first things first and just take a few minutes every morning to be with Him. Have you allowed your life to become so busy that you have forced God out?

Final Word

Jesus is coming back. No one knows exactly when, but His Second Coming is as certain as His first coming was. It will be the most exciting day on earth when Jesus returns but only for those who are prepared. At the start of this book, I asked the question, "Are there modern-day prophets?" In one sense, as this world winds down prior to Jesus's Second Coming, I believe all true believers will function as modern-day prophets. It will be our job to do the following:

- Warn unbelievers of what is coming, hoping they will turn to God.
- Encourage other believers to maintain their faith in God.
- Pray and fast as we have never done before, in order to partner with God in His restoration of all things.

The ancient path is a path with an eternal destination. The prophets of old told us to get on the path and stay on it. Nothing has changed!

CPSIA information can be obtained
at www.ICGtesting.com
Printed in the USA
LVHW05s1609260718
585000LV00004BA/74/P